From Spark to Flame

Fanning Your Passion & Ideas into Moneymaking Magazine Articles that Make a Difference

by W. Bradford Swift

Porpoise Publishing

Flat Rock, NC 28731
www.lifeonpurpose.com
Library of Congress Cataloging-in-Publication Data

Swift, W. Bradford
From Spark to Flame : Fanning Your Passion & Ideas into
Moneymaking Magazine Articles that Make a Difference / W.
Bradford Swift.
p. cm.
ISBN-978-1-93032-808-2 (softcover)
ISBN-10: 1-93032-808-7 (softcover)
1. Writing for magazines 2. Purposeful writing 3. Writing for
money 4. Freelance writer 5. Journalism. I. Title.

Cover photo by Joe Benjamin
Author's photo by B. J. Condrey

Typesetting by Ann T. Swift
Edited by Marilyn Noble

Typeset in Palatina
Printed in USA
First Edition

"Words do not label things already there. Words are like the knife of the carver: They free the idea, the thing, from the general formlessness of the outside. As a man speaks, not only is his language in a state of birth, but also the very thing about which he is talking." -- Old Eskimo saying

Dedication

I dedicate this book to Mrs. Crabtree. The children's librarian that lived next door to my family when I was growing up. She took pity on my mom as she struggled to raise two rambunctious boys on her own. One day Mrs. Crabtree dropped a stack of books hand picked for a boy my age. They sat on the table next to my bed for several days like a loaded trap. Finally, from utter boredom I picked one up and started reading. The rest is history. Thanks Mrs. Crabtree for caring.

Acknowledgments

I want to acknowledge the dozens of editors and their assistants who helped me learn the craft of writing, as well as the members of the Visionary Writers On Purpose Team who proved to me that the Writers Taffy Machine approach outlined in this book could work for other writers as well as it's worked for me.

I am also eternally grateful to the two lovely ladies of my life – my wife and soulmate, Ann, and my talented daughter, Amber. Without you, all the efforts of writing a book would hardly be worth it.

And thanks to Marilyn Noble for editing the book, Joe Benjamin for the "sparkling" cover photo and B. J. Condrey for her photo of Little Bit and me.

Table of Contents

Introduction

Have you ever read a magazine article and thought to yourself, "Why, I could have written that article!" or, "I could have written a *better* article than that!" You're probably right. I know I've read many articles that elicited similar thoughts.

You might be like a lot of aspiring writers I've talked to through the years who know they have the talent to be writers. Perhaps people have read something you wrote and told you how well it was written. Or maybe you simply have a deep yearning to see your thoughts, feelings, and ideas in print, along with your name. Or perhaps you've a deep desire to contribute to others through the written word, believing that indeed "the pen is mightier than the sword." But, like many aspiring writers, you may not know how to turn your ideas into articles — especially articles that magazines will buy.

This book, like my workshop with the same name, is purely and simply about how to turn your ideas into moneymaking magazine articles, but with an added twist - magazine articles that make a difference in the world and allow you, the author, to express your purpose and passion. If you're someone who would like to see your name as a byline for some of the thousands of articles that are written each year, this book is for you. You may want to do it as a paying hobby, you may just want to give it a shot to see if you can get one article published (although I'll warn you, seeing your name in print can be addictive), or you may want to develop a career as a part-time or full-time freelance writer. Wherever you fit along that gradient, this book will detail how to go from being an aspiring writer to a published and profitable writer.

I've taught these concepts in a workshop setting to hundreds of aspiring writers through the years. At this point, if we were in my workshop, I would ask you to close your eyes for a brief guided visualization. So take a moment to read the following instructions, and then allow yourself to get into the experience.

The Magic of the Mail

Imagine you've already learned everything possible from this book, and you've applied the principles and followed the advice for the past six months. Over this half-year, you've become a "mail-watcher," a sure sign you're heading down the path of being a writer. The arrival of the mail has become a cherished moment, one filled with anticipation, but usually followed by disappointment.

Today, you take the mail from your box and rummage through the mound of circulars and bills, looking for that special envelope. But today is different from all of those other days because at the bottom of the pile is a letter you don't recognize. You stare at it for a moment, unsure whether or not you're seeing things or if that envelope you've been waiting for is really in your hands. Finally, with fingers trembling, you tear it open.

Take a few moments to imagine opening your mail and finding that special envelope addressed to you from one of the magazines you've contacted over the past six months. Then turn the page to see what's inside...

```
Top Magazine USA                                              1101
111 Anywhere St.
New York NY 11011


Pay To The
Order Of: _____YOU _____        $1200.00

***Twelve Hundred Dollars and No Cents*** US Dollars


Memo: Fantastically Written Article    Signature____ Edward D. Editor  ____
87769966    69696969-000
```

     In the twenty-plus years I've been writing and getting paid for my work, the thrill of receiving a check hasn't diminished. Does that mean I write only for the money? Hardly! You'll find that there are many, much easier ways to make a living — like practicing veterinary medicine, my first profession for more than fifteen years. I sold my practice to pursue my second dream career as a writer, speaker, and personal coach. I know of few occupations that are more fulfilling, satisfying, or fun than being a published writer. But I'm going to encourage you to become more than just a writer, more than just a freelance journalist. I'm going to encourage you to become a "Writer On Purpose." In other words, why not use your gift of writing as a way to express your purpose in life, and in the process, write articles that contribute to and make a difference for others? So, if you'd like to experience the thrill of that first check, knowing that it represents a difference being made in the world, read on as we explore the magical profession, hobby, and pastime of being a Writer On Purpose.

This book is for "aspiring magazine writers." That means it's for people who yearn to write and publish what they write in national and regional magazines. While I won't directly address writing for newspapers, much of the information is applicable. This book isn't about getting your works of fiction published, although again, much of the information could be applied there as well. Our focus will be on nonfiction writing and how you can fan the sparks of your passion and ideas into moneymaking magazine articles that make a difference.

Before we begin, I think it would be valuable for you to know a little more about my own journey. As I've said, before becoming a writer, I was a veterinarian, with my own small-animal practice in High Point, North Carolina.

In 1984, I began hearing about a new computer called the Macintosh. Being an Apple computer enthusiast, I decided one Saturday to visit the local Apple store and check out this new toy. Twenty minutes later, thanks to a nice sales lady, I strolled out with my own Macintosh, a printer, and a new credit card with the entire purchase on the account.

My Macintosh was one of the first 1,000 machines off the assembly line, and only two programs were available for it — MacPaint and MacWrite. It didn't take long for me to realize it's next to impossible to draw anything useful with a mouse. Fun, yes. Useful, no. By Monday morning, with a good case of buyer's remorse setting in, I became frantic to find some way to justify this irrational and spontaneous buying spree. Finally, I decided the Macintosh was a sign. After all, I had been telling myself for years that one day I would try my hand at writing. After glancing at the calendar and my charge card bill, I realized that one day had arrived.

I set about writing my first article, a short piece about the reasons for spaying your cat, which I promptly sent off to *Purrrrr!* (I remember to this day that the title of the magazine is spelled with five R's), a newsletter for cat lovers published in Maine. A month or so later, I received my first check in the mail for $50. I was thrilled and delighted. Next, I wrote a long short story, "Dog's Best Friend," a science fiction story loosely taken from my experiences with the then new Parvovirus. I dashed it off to a small science fiction magazine for young adults, which promptly sent me back an acceptance.

Wow! I was batting two for two. My impression was that this writing thing was going to be a breeze. I started envisioning a life of leisure, sitting on the deck of my mountain hideaway, typing a couple hours each day on my next best seller.

"Dog's Best Friend" gave me my first exposure to the difference between "paid on acceptance" and "paid on publication." A magazine accepted my short story as "paid on publication," which meant that, although they had accepted my story, I would not get paid until they printed it. After waiting eighteen months with no check, despite numerous letters reminding them of their promise, I grew impatient. By this time I had become a regular contributor to *Purrrrr!* They published all the articles I sent to them and paid me right away. So, I figured, I would just take "Dog's Best Friend" back and get it published somewhere else, probably for more money than I had been offered. That's what I did.

That was more than twenty years ago, and "Dog's Best Friend" has yet to find its way into print. During the same time span, I also learned that the business of writing isn't always quite as easy as those early beginner's luck experiences suggested. At the same time, I've discovered a lot about what works and what doesn't in the world of magazine publishing. This book is the essence of those experiences.

The Power Of Coaching

I believe one of the most powerful and effective ways to present what I've learned is through "coaching." Therefore, consider me your writing coach. In each chapter, we'll cover certain fundamentals of the game of "Writing Magazine Articles for Money." My job, as your coach, is to improve your performance in this game. Your job is to accept the coaching that fits for you and apply it on the field of play.

If you read this book without following or trying any of the ideas or exercises, you'll be wasting your time. The most effective coaching will result from your doing the assignments at the end of each chapter. The assignments are not only fun, but they're designed to make you a published, paid writer. So if you're serious about that, accept this first piece of coaching:

DO THE ASSIGNMENTS!

Now, let's get started by looking at how to build the writer's Taffy Machine.

Chapter 1
The Writers Taffy Machine

Growing up, one of my favorite places to spend summer vacation was along the coast of North Carolina at Atlantic Beach, and one of my fondest memories is of watching the automatic taffy-pulling machine. Into one end of this magical machine the owner would pour the ingredients for making taffy that, of course, included a lot of sugar. He would then turn the machine on and after a few minutes, it would begin churning out multi-colored strands of taffy, ready to be boxed and sold to a line of salivating children, including me.

Because of that cherished memory, I now have upon my office wall what I call my "Writer's Taffy Machine." At one end I pour in the sweet blend of ideas and passion, while the other end churns out checks from magazine publishers. Between these two ends are all the steps we'll cover in detail in this book.

By the time you finish reading, you'll know how to build a writer's taffy machine, and, if you accept the coaching and do the assignments, you'll be well on your way to building one for yourself.

At this point, ask yourself a couple of important questions:

- Am I interested in building my own taffy machine?

- Will I do the necessary work to maintain my machine and have it churn out moneymaking magazine articles?

Take a few moments now and answer these questions for yourself. Then, get a notebook or journal to use in conjunction with this book and make your first entry a written statement of what you intend to accomplish from our working together through this book. Be as specific as possible. If you're unsure whether or not you're ready to commit to doing the work, that's fair. Write that down. This is just a starting point, and you can always revise your intentions later. I encourage you to stretch beyond what you think you can accomplish. Remember, part of my job as your writing coach is to improve your performance beyond what you can accomplish on your own.

Now, let's look at the components of a Writer's Taffy Machine— the machine that turns your ideas into money. What are some of the steps between your sweet ideas and the even sweeter checks?

Blueprint for Building Your Taffy Machine

Every article starts with an idea. One of the question writers hear most from aspiring writers is, "Where do you get your ideas?" One of the most talented and prolific writers I've ever met, Harlan Ellison, would often facetiously answer such a question by replying, "Why, I buy them from a man in Poughkeepsie. Ten ideas for ten bucks."

But even before asking the "where" question, I suggest looking more deeply at some "why" questions. Why are you writing? Even more important, why are you here? In Chapter 2 we'll explore the vital importance of purpose for writers. While one purpose for writing is to make money, I'm going to suggest it's simply not enough. After all, there are far easier ways to make money, and a lot more of it than most people ever make writing. Now, I'm not saying you can't make a good living as a freelance writer. What I am saying that spending some time to become clear what your purpose is for writing and how it ties in with your greater life purpose will make all the difference in your writing, and in your life. In fact, a clear sense of purpose will act like a magnet that will attract to you the perfect ideas to develop into money making magazine articles.

Following most chapters are suggested ways to put what you've just learned into action in your writing life. It's completely up to you as to how many of these suggestions you take. As your writing coach, I must tell you that the more suggestions you take, the more impact this book will have on your writing. These suggestions will work, if you work.

Ready to get started? To begin, we'll examine how you can use the flint and metal of passion and ideas to ignite your sparks and get you on your way to writing powerful and entertaining magazine articles that sell.

Call to Action Assignment
Create your own Writer's Taffy Machine, or its equivalent. You might decide that your 'system' will be a flower garden, with ideas being the seeds you're

planting. Or you could work with a stream metaphor, with the ideas being fish making their way from the small mountain pond down to the ocean (where they turn into checks). I recommend using a corkboard that's at least 24 by 36 inches, displayed on a wall in the area you've designated for your writing. Use either the blank backs of old business cards, or cut 3 by 5 inch note cards in half or thirds. Use a new card for each new idea you find.

Writer's Taffy Machine Display

Top Ideas	Idea Development	Query & Mag. Select	Mail Out	Phone Followup	No Yes
Payments	Submissions	Revisions	Rough Drafts	Research	Outline & Questions

Chapter 2
Writing on Purpose with Passion and Play

What's your life purpose? Relax, I know that can be quite a heady question. I also know that for many writers, the answer might be "to write." I'd like to invite you to try on a different perspective. While the entire process of clarifying your life purpose is beyond the scope of this book, you can consider this chapter as a crash course in getting started. For a proven, systematic approach to clarifying your life purpose pick up a copy of my book, *Life On Purpose: Six Passages to an Inspired Life.* (www.lifeonpurpose.com/books)

You may be asking what this has to do with writing money making magazine articles. My response is EVERYTHING, because without a clear sense of purpose, your writing career and your writing will be missing the passion that turns so-so writing into the type of writing editors are willing to pay good money for. And let's face it, making a living as a writer isn't always that easy. In fact, most professional freelancers would probably say it's NEVER that easy. Without a clear sense of purpose, it's too easy to get discouraged and end up throwing in the towel. But the clearer you are that your writing is an expression of your true purpose for being on planet earth, the more unstoppable you become.

Now, let's look at a couple different perspectives of life purpose – the cultural perspective, what most people would say a life purpose is, and the Life On Purpose Perspective.

The Cultural Perspective

Over the years I've surveyed thousands of people asking them one simple question: "What is a life purpose?" While I've received many interesting answers, the most interesting observation is that the vast majority of the responses had this common theme: "A life purpose is what I'm here to **do** during my life." What that equates to is that most people consider their purpose in life as either their job, career, or profession such as writer, corporate executive, or physician. Or they may consider their life purpose to be some significant role they play, like being a good parent, a good employee, or community member.

But I'd like to offer you a different perspective; one that many people have found to be key to enhancing their life. Consider that a life purpose could also be viewed as **the context, vessel or container into which you pour your life.** In other words it's a context for your life that then shapes your life and all that you do. Not just your career, not just the important roles of your life, but each and every moment. When you look at your life from this Life On Purpose Perspective, then it's possible to be living true to your life purpose in all of your life, not just when you're writing, not just when you're being a parent, but each and every moment. This doesn't mean that your writing, your parenting, and all the other things you do aren't important. They are! Your job, your roles in life, everything you do become the various ways you express your true purpose.

For example, while I still spend a lot of my time writing, I also spend time as the founder of Life On Purpose Institute, as a life purpose coach, as a husband and a dad. But none of these activities is my life purpose. My life purpose, the context that gives shape and form to each of these activities is to live an inspired and inspiring life of purposeful, passionate and playful service, a life of mindful abundance balanced with simplicity, and spiritual serenity.

Living a life of service, simplicity, and spiritual serenity becomes the vessel into which I pour my life. The result is that not only do I experience such a life, but my actions become an expression of my life purpose. Before moving on from the Purposeful Path, there is one other point that's too important not to touch on, and that's the relationship between purpose, passion, and play.

Purpose, Passion and Play

When you're clear what your true purpose is in life, you're then able to use that purpose to tap into a wellspring of passionate energy that then propels your forward in all the different ways you choose to express your purpose, including your writing.

You may be thinking at this point, "But can't I get published writing about something I am not passionate about and doesn't have anything to do with my purpose in life?"

The answer, of course, is yes. I've done it, and

the stories were published. In fact, those experiences enabled me to understand the importance of identifying and writing about topics that I *am* passionate about. And what I discovered is that I want to write— as often as possible— about topics that fuel my passions.

The hard lesson I learned about passion came fairly early in my freelance career. I had sold my veterinary practice and was striving to become stable and profitable as a full-time freelance writer specializing in writing magazine articles. At the time I lived in Greensboro, North Carolina, which was also the home of a magazine publisher of an in-flight magazine. Because I lived close by, I mustered up enough nerve to visit the editor, a nice woman named Maggie Oman. This was my first face-to-face meeting with a magazine editor, and I was nervous as a groom standing at the altar.

Maggie must have picked up on this and made it a point to be gentle and cordial, so I survived the meeting without any undo embarrassment. After that, I started sending her ideas for possible articles. After sending four or five different ideas, I received a call from Maggie, offering me an assignment. She told me that she liked my writing style but that none of the ideas quite hit the mark. She did, however, need a piece on the trend of business suites. I didn't know much, nor did I care much, about business suites, but I figured an assignment was an assignment. After all, I didn't have a long line of other assignments. I could use the money, which was good, and the clip, which was even better. (A clip is a copy of a published article you've written. You include copies of your clips in future queries to other magazines to show editors that you can, indeed, write well enough to be published.)

I took the assignment. I worked hard on it, interviewed a lot of suite experts, and turned in what I thought was a credible article. Before too long, I received a check in the mail and a new assignment.

This one was on office technology. I love gadgets, so the subject was fairly interesting. I wrote it, received the check, and a new assignment. This went on for four or five different articles, each one business related, and each one less and less interesting. The worst one I remember was about office furniture. Even though I lived within thirty minutes of High Point, North Carolina, the furniture capital of the world, I had no passion for the subject. But I took the assignment anyway and churned out another article.

What I didn't realize at the time was that my lack of interest about the subjects was having a grave effect on the quality of my work. In short, the articles I submitted were poorly written. I hadn't bothered to look at the published articles, or I would have seen that they were being heavily edited by one of the magazine editors prior to publication. I was too busy for such nonsense, not to mention that by the time I finished the articles, I was bored to tears with whatever the subject had been.

After finishing the last assignment, several weeks went by without a word from Maggie. True, I hated working on those articles, but I needed the money. I finally called her and in my most pleasant, up-beat voice said, "Hi, Maggie, I'm calling for my next assignment. What do you have?"

There was a long pause on the other end of the line before Maggie replied, "Well, frankly, Brad, there won't be any other assignments." She then went on to describe in some detail how far short my articles had fallen. She told me that she'd kept hoping I would learn from their editing efforts what they were looking for, but since I hadn't shown any inclination in that direction, she felt it would be unwise for the relationship to continue.

I was devastated, although deep inside, I wasn't surprised. Somehow I knew I wasn't putting forth my best effort, just the best I could muster for topics that sparked no passion in me. It was one of the most important lessons I learned in those early days.

Do I still take assignments that I am less than passionate about? Yes, once in a while, but not without knowing the dangerous ground on which I'm treading. In those cases, I make it a point to find something about the article that does interest me, something about which I can generate a bit of enthusiasm. And I strive to keep such assignments to a minimum by always having a lot of great passionate ideas circulating to many different magazines.

Igniting Passion through Purpose

Why so much emphasis on passion? There are several reasons. Writing about subjects that interest you and ignite your passion is a whole lot more fun, and the articles are easier to write. Besides, the final product is likely to be much better.

A few years ago I discovered that I'm passionate about writing profiles, interviews, and other kinds of articles about people who are committed to making a difference in the world. I had also determined by that time that the whole subject of purpose was part of my life purpose, so in an effort to bring more purpose and meaning to my writing career, I created Project Purpose:

To write and publish articles about people and institutions whose lives and missions are dedicated to a bold and inspired purpose or vision.

I started to focus my efforts on getting assignments that would fit Project Purpose. About three months after creating the project, I received my first official Project Purpose assignment to write a profile of Bo Lozoff of The Human Kindness Foundation in Carrboro, North Carolina. The assignment came from *New Age Journal* (since re-named *Body and Soul*). At the time, it was the largest assignment I'd received, both in the prestige of the magazine and the size of the paycheck. In fact, the check was close to double what I had so far received for any other single article.

Perhaps the most interesting phenomenon was that receiving the payment was the proverbial icing on the cake. I loved doing the research for the article, which involved traveling to Carborro to interview Bo, his wife, Sita, and other people whose lives had been touched by this incredible couple.

The writing was a joy, both challenging and fun. Even the revision process was virtually painless because I was doing something close to my heart.

Then the check arrived — the icing on an already delectable dessert, and I knew I had hit upon something really important. As Greg Braendel of Career Dreams, Inc. and another Project Purpose profile subject says, "Passion always sells, obsession never does."

The other reason I encourage aspiring writers to tap into their passions is because the profession of freelance writing is a tough one. There's a lot of competition. Busy, often over-worked editors are not always as nice as they could be. And the pay . . . well, there are easier ways to make money, as I've said. I've seen and talked to too many freelancers, both part-timers and those doing it for a living, who have become jaded about their work. In many cases, that happens because they sell out by writing too many articles that they find boring and uninteresting just to pay the rent. They find subjects they can write about that, even though uninspiring, still bring in the bacon. But years of writing just for the money can desiccate the staunchest soul. Don't let it happen to you.

Tapping Into Your Passion

What stirs your passion? The question isn't as silly as you may think. Many people have lost touch with their passion, the inner spark that ignites them into inspired action. The best they can muster is a mild curiosity or a passing interest.

The following exercise will help you get in touch with your passion and help determine what's really important to you. I recommend that you take out your notebook and find a nice quiet place to go through this exercise. Find a place where you can be sure you won't be disturbed during the short time the exercise will take. Here's the set up:

The Passion Police are on the way to your home. In just a few minutes, they'll knock on your door. Their mission is to take away everything you're passionate about. Your only hope is to write down those things in life that are really important to you. If it's not written down, the Passion Police will take it away, never to be in your world again.

You must be as precise as possible about what you write. For instance, if relationships are important to you, write down which relationships are important. If you're passionate about nature, write down the specific aspects of nature that matter the most to you. If you love animals, which ones do you love most? Describe the specific details of your passion. What do you want to have in your world after the Passion Police leave? It must be written down or, after they've left, it won't exist in your world.

They're almost at your door. You now have five minutes to record in your notebook everything that you're passionate about. Check your watch and start writing. Remember — five minutes of writing as much and as fast and as precisely as you can. BEGIN!

How did you do?

It's likely that as you look over your list you'll realized you missed some important things that you want in your world. Okay, take one minute and add those to your list. The passion police were a little slow today. Once you've made those additions, look over the list again. While you may not have listed everything you're passionate about, it's a great place to start getting ideas you could write about.

Purposefully Playing with Your Writing

Is it really possible to make a living doing something you love and have a lot of fun in the process? YES -- if you set your intention to purposefully play with the ways you express your life purpose. The secret to purposeful play is to not get overly attached to the results you're out to produce. While it may sound paradoxical, it's possible to be committed to your writing career while at the same time not taking it too seriously. When you stay committed and unattached, you'll probably find you're much more effective at producing results. Now that's a paradox worth grappling with.

Call to Action Assignment

Continue to add to your Passion List. Add things that mean a lot to you as well as things that you find interesting or that you're curious about. Then, from that list, make a top 10 list of what you're most passionate about. Keep this list visible where you write.

Chapter 3
The Spark of Passion-Filled Ideas

Ideas are the raw material for your writer's taffy machine. The more passion-filled ideas you collect, the more sweet articles you can write, the more difference you can make, and the more money you can earn. In this chapter, we'll look at some of great places you can find ideas.

Before we start, consider this. Ideas for magazine articles are common property, so while you want to be sure you're igniting your work by writing about topics you're passionate about, you don't have to worry about the ideas being just yours. Since you can't copyright an idea, you can borrow them from other people, even from other material you read.

"Isn't that plagiarism?" you ask. Not as long as you just borrow the ideas and not the particular words the author used. So one great place to find ideas for your Writer's Taffy Machine is:

The Media

This includes television, radio, newspapers, newsletters, and the Internet. For example, the first piece I wrote for *Omni Magazine* was about the magic of the tobacco plant. The idea came from a short article that appeared in the local newspaper. Since I live in North Carolina, the tobacco plant is big news, especially when researchers find two separate ways to use it in a beneficial way.

The newspaper article explained how researchers were utilizing the tobacco plant to produce anti-AIDS and anti-cancer drugs. This research, coupled with additional information on extracting edible vegetable protein from the tobacco plant, suggested that one day in the not-too-distant future tobacco may be primarily grown for purposes other than smoking.

The basic information for my query letter came from the newspaper article. Subsequently, I turned that idea into a $800 assignment from a magazine I had been trying to break into for several months.

Newsletters

Newsletters are a popular way many organizations use stay in touch with their members, and they can be a source of new ideas for a writer. I often get requests from local kennel clubs for permission to reprint an article I've written on some canine subject. Because most of these clubs operate on a very small budget and have a small circulation, I usually don't ask a fee for such reprinting. I do request that the organization place me on their newsletter mailing list. I did this a few years ago for a small Doberman pinscher newsletter. In the first issue I received was a short letter about Chitra Besbroda and her nonprofit organization, Sentient Creatures, Inc. The story recounted that Chitra was a woman on a mission to save as many of the "junkyard dogs" of Harlem as possible. These are dogs that, according to Besbroda, are used as living burglar alarms to guard rundown buildings in Harlem. Unfortunately, many of them are mistreated, underfed, and ignored. I was touched by the story and contacted Chitra for more information.

Before long, I developed an article and placed her story in *Animals Magazine,* for just under $500. Not bad for an idea from a free newsletter. Even better is that since then, her story has appeared in at least two other publications, both with my byline -- and, of course, that means my name was on two other checks.

Public Relations Firms

A public relations firm's job is to get its clients known in a positive light by the public. Because one of my specialties is writing inspiring stories about people making a difference in the world, I view PR people as my allies in this endeavor. It was through such a firm that I met Greg Braendel, the founder and president of Career Dreams, Inc. It was a match made in heaven. Greg, a former actor, had run a successful manufacturing and distribution company for, of all things, toilet partitions. As Greg says, "Somebody had to make them." But the ones that Greg's company sold were designed in England and were better than anything else in this country. His company grew from a $10,000 investment into a $10 million company in just three years before he sold it. He then spent the next few years trying to figure out how they had been so successful. What he gleaned from that investigation became the nucleus of his new company, or CDI. CDI's premise is that we're all brilliant at something and that when we can identify our brilliance and our God-given talents, we can then find or create a job that allows us to utilize these talents to our fullest.

Not only did I find it easy to place Greg's story in a major magazine, but in the process Greg and I hit it off so well that we collaborated on a book about the successes of CDI. Yes, PR agents are my friends.

Personal Experience And Interests

Of course, we all have a wealth of great story ideas right at our fingertips, or more accurately, within our own memory and experiences. As a veterinarian, I've been able to write hundreds of different stories that have come from my training and experience. I often needed to do additional research, but the ideas themselves came straight from my life. Everywhere I go and everyone I meet is a potential next story.

A few years ago, just as I was beginning to work on Project Purpose, I attended a retreat in nearby Black Mountain. That's where I met Bo Lozoff, co-director the Human Kindness Foundation. As the keynote speaker, Bo gave two talks, both of which blew me away because of his power and authenticity. I heard myself thinking, *This man's message needs a much larger audience.* I knew I had my next story. As it's turned out, I've written three different articles about Bo and the work he does with prisoners through his prison-ashram project. One of those articles has been reprinted in three different magazines in three different languages. It's a beneficial relationship for both of us. Not only did I more than recoup the cost of the original retreat many times over, but it's fulfilling to know that thousands more people know about Bo and his work through my efforts. Such win-win-win relationships are common occurrences when your writing is focused by your passion and purpose.

From Other Articles

Sometimes your next idea will come from an article you're already working on, as happened to me while I was writing a feature story for *Yoga Journal* on simple living in a complex world. One of the people I interviewed for the piece was noted environmentalist and author John Robbins. Besides being well known for his best selling book, *Diet For A New America*, John is also known as the heir who walked away from the Baskin-Robbins ice cream fortune.

While interviewing John for the *Yoga Journal* article, he mentioned he was working on a new book, *Reclaiming Our Health*, and that it was to be an expose of the American Medical Association. I asked him a few more questions about the book and found out that it would be out later that year. Then we went on with the interview, but not before I had jotted down a few comments about the new book on a note card. Within a few months I had a second article assignment from *Yoga Journal*, this time an interview piece on John Robbins and his new book.

But the story doesn't stop there. While working on the article, I had to send some of the material to John for his approval through email. John's son, Ocean, is the Robbin's family computer wiz, and he helped me get the files to John in a readable fashion. And, in passing, Ocean sent me a copy of his own book and a short biography. It was an impressive bio for a young man of 22:

- participated in his first peace demonstration at the age of 7
- ran his first marathon at 10, the same year he started his first business, Ocean's Natural Bakery
- served as an emissary for the U.S. on two different trips to Russia
- started his own nonprofit organization at the age of 16

Sure enough, within a few weeks, I had my next assignment to write about this untroubled youth for *Hope Magazine*.

Recruit Roving Reporters
I learned about Norman Vaughan from a newspaper clipping I received from one of my roving reporters. I created a group of "rovers" around the country to read the material they were already accustomed to reading — their local newspapers, newsletters, and magazines — and to look for interesting people for me to profile in national magazines. When an idea strikes home, like the Vaughan story, I pay the rover a percentage of the income that I earn from the article.

The year I interviewed Vaughan, he and his wife Carolyn were planning a trip to climb a mountain that had been named after him several years previously. Mount Vaughan had been given its name by the explorer Admiral Byrd during his first trip to the bottom of the world, Antarctica. Vaughan had dropped out of Harvard to accompany Byrd on the expedition. (Imagine what his parents must have thought.)

The trip was just the start of an incredible life of adventure, culminating in his trip up Mount Vaughan. The Vaughans finally made it to the top of Mount Vaughan where they celebrated Norman's birthday — his 89th. Not a bad way to spend a birthday. I managed to place his story in a number of different publications, which I imagine made fundraising for trips in the future just a little bit easier.

These are just a few of the many different ways to collect ideas to feed into your Writer's Taffy Machine. Ideas are everywhere when you begin looking at the world as a freelance writer. With a little practice it won't be long before you're not only collecting dozens of new ideas every week, but also developing a sixth sense about which ideas are likely to turn into assignments.

One of the most important ways to be sure you always have more great ideas to write about than you'll ever actually write is to have a simple way to capture the ideas when they cross your path. I've two favorite methods. I keep a small memo pad and pen with me at all times. As soon as I stumble upon something I can use for an article, I jot it down. The second system makes good use of old, out-dated business cards. Turn them over and use the blank back to jot down article ideas. This last method works especially well for me because the ideas are ready to be tacked onto the corkboard of my Writer's Taffy

Machine. My view is that an idea not captured quickly turns into somebody else's idea, so I make it a point to put them in writing.

Ideas are a writer's raw material; the more you've got, the more masterpieces you'll create. If this isn't clear now, it will be as we continue exploring the process of the Writer's Taffy Machine.

Making It Real

At this point you probably understand conceptually that it makes good sense for a writer to constantly keep the nets out for new ideas. For this to make any real difference in your writing efforts, you must now take it from the realm of concept to the realm of action. In other words, we need to turn the coaching into reality.

Call to Action Assignment

1. Make a game of collecting ideas. Set a target for yourself; say 100 ideas collected within the next month or twenty five new ideas written down this week. Decide which game would be a stretch, but still something you can accomplish. Then play the game full out during the time you set.

2. Determine what structure you'll use to collect your ideas. Will it be on note cards, a small notepad you can keep with you, the back of old business cards, or some combination of different methods? Experiment with this until you develop the system that works best for you. Remember, collecting ideas is just part of the process. You also want to have easy access to the ideas you collect.

3. Begin to notice which ideas really excite you. See if a pattern begins to emerge. It may suggest a specialty you would enjoy developing.

4. Once a week sit down with an empty pad of paper and write down as many ideas as possible that come to you in fifteen minutes. Look back over the previous week to see if you met anyone you might want to write about or if you observed anything that interested you. How could you turn that into an article? Don't worry about whether the ideas are any good or not; just write them down as fast as they come to you. You can go back later and select the ones you would like to develop.

Chapter 4 -- The Market:
The Common Ground Between
Passion and Ideas

In our last chapter, we considered how important it is to write on purpose with passion and play. To keep our Taffy Machine in balance, we're now going to the other end of the spectrum to take a look at the market, and the connection between your ideas and where you plan to place them. The market is a general term that encompasses all the possible places where you might sell your articles. While the focus of this book is regional and national magazines, most of the principles will apply to other markets such as newspapers and the Internet.

Many experienced writers will tell an aspiring writer that if you want to make it in this profession, you must figure out what the market is looking for and provide it. I agree . . . to a degree.

While your articles must fit into whatever magazines you desire to write for, you can also write from your passion and find many magazines that will support you in that endeavor. A favorite quote of mine from Frederick Buechner demonstrates what I mean:

"Where your deep gladness meets with the deep hunger of the world, there you'll find a further calling."

Writing magazine articles about passion-filled topics is half the equation. The other half is finding markets with a deep hunger for what you're offering. In other words, it's important to find a happy medium, somewhere between your passion and what the market is looking for.

Fortunately, there's plenty of room in this middle ground, especially with hundreds of special interest magazines now available.

Since I began working on Project Purpose around 1995, I've made it a favorite pastime to find new markets for these types of articles. Not all of them pan out, but I'm constantly looking because I know that the more markets I can find, the more flexibility I have in writing about this passion of mine. During this time I've been privileged to meet and interview some remarkable people with amazing stories.

Now that you're beginning to pour the raw materials of great ideas into your Writer's Taffy Machine, let's look to see where they go next.

The Developing Chamber

The developing chamber is where each idea can be blended, kneaded, and molded into the makings of a magazine article. But while the ideas are beginning to be molded, a second process must also be underway. That's determining where you're going to send the idea once it's ready. In this way, you begin to customize your ideas to be a perfect fit for one or more magazines.

At this point in the process, you need to begin looking from two different perspectives. The first perspective, already discussed, is what are you passionate about? That's one side of the equation. On the other side is the question, "What kinds of article ideas are magazines interested in receiving?" Of course, the answer to that question depends on the magazine. There are so many magazines, and so many new ones popping up every day while others are closing their doors, that knowing where to send your ideas isn't simple. This abundance of magazines is good news for aspiring writers, but it can also be a bit overwhelming.

Where do you start? What magazines take freelance submissions and which are staff written? Which ones take the types of article ideas you're interested in developing? To whom do you send the ideas? What do they pay and when? The questions are close to endless.

Relax! The questions you're asking are the same questions most aspiring writers have at this point. And we're going to find the answers together.

You now have an equation with one side consisting of the ideas you're passionate about developing into articles and the other side consisting of what the market is looking for. Somewhere in the middle are the ideas that get written, sold, and published.

PASSION-POWERED IDEAS <= SOLD ARTICLES=> HUNGRY MARKET NEEDS

Since we've done a fair amount of work on the "Passion-Powered Idea" side of the equation, let's look a little closer at the "Hungry Market Needs" side.

Imagine yourself as a matchmaker. Your job is to match up passion-powered ideas with hungry markets looking for those kinds of ideas to offer up to their readers.

With thousands of potential markets, how do you go about deciding where to submit your ideas? Market research will help oil your machine to produce successful articles — articles that sell.

We'll start by using a "Heart List" to narrow your focus to a workable size.

Hit The Mark With Your Heart List

A Heart List is a selection of magazines in which you would love to see your article and byline. You may place a magazine on your list because they pay well, because you've enjoyed reading the magazine for years, because of their prestigious reputation, because of the far-reaching circulation, or for all these reasons or any combination. While your Heart List can be any size, I've found that for most aspiring writers, a list of from ten to twenty five different magazines is a good working size. Now, let's look a little closer to see how to select the magazines for your list.

The easiest place to start is with the magazines you read on a regular basis. After all, you're reading them because there's something about the editorial content that you enjoy. Don't worry at this point if you suddenly have a flash of inferiority and you hear yourself saying, "I could never write for *Vanity Fair*, or *National Geographic*, or _____ [fill-in-the-blank]."

Maybe you can; maybe you can't. That's not what should concern you right now. Instead, ask, "If I could write for any magazines, which ones would they be?"

You can narrow the choices down a little further by asking these additional questions:

- Which magazines are likely to be interested in the ideas from your growing list of possible articles?
- Which magazines pay a decent rate for their articles? (We'll discuss how to find out this information a little later.)
- What are some top-notch national publications where you'd love to see your byline?
- How about some mid-range publications that might be more open to new writers? How about local or regional magazines?
- Are there some trade magazines or journals that would be open and receptive to the kinds of ideas you want to write about?

Trade magazines usually aren't found on the newsstands, but are connected with a profession, career or trade. The good news is that often times trade publications pay well and can be fun to work with. For example, for over a decade I've written for *Veterinary Economics*, a trade magazine from my former career as a veterinarian. It was my favorite vet-related publication to read on a regular basis when I was in practice, and I enjoy writing articles ranging in scope from how to create a practice on purpose (one of my favorite themes), to how to build a strong business by building a strong team. And to top it off, the return on the time I invest to produce a well-written article is worthwhile.

It may be necessary to make some trips to the library and a large magazine newsstand for market research. That's right, now that you've become a writer, an afternoon browsing through the magazine racks has suddenly been transformed into a business afternoon of market research. Nifty, huh?

Today, one of the best places to conduct your market research is through the Internet. Most magazines have their own Web sites and many of them keep back issues or portions of back issues online.

Whether your research is conducted in a library, bookstore, magazine store, or online, there are some additional things you'll want to do on these market research days.

First, take a pen and pad with you to jot down any notes. You'll probably run across some magazines you want to buy so you have a recent issue to study, but there will be others that look interesting but aren't necessarily a good investment of your money. Their content may have limited appeal to you, or you may not be sure if it's a paying market.

In this case, jot down the magazine's name, address, phone number, the name of the editor, and the Web site or email address. Later you can send a letter or email to the magazine requesting a copy of their writers' guidelines. Additionally, many magazines now carry their guidelines online at their Web sites, so you can find them there. While not all guidelines go into detail about pay for freelancers, many of them will give you enough of an idea to determine if the magazine is right for your Heart List.

Another great place to find information about new magazines that you may want to add to your Heart List is *Writer's Market,* a publication of Writer's Digest. Most freelance journalists consider *Writer's Market* to be the Bible for publishing information, with thousands of magazine, book publisher and agent listings. It's well worth the thirty dollar investment, and you can also register to receive the same information from the writersmarket.com Web site.

Begin training your eye to study the magazines carefully. Is it a slick publication with plenty of color photos, printed on a high quality paper, or is it less-expensively produced? Study the ads to get a better sense of the slant and readership of the magazine. For instance, what is the income bracket of its readers and their age range? Are they male or female, or both? Does the magazine have a balance of features and departmental pieces? Do authors have a tagline at the end of the article with a short explanation of their credentials? If so, read through a few to see how many articles were written by freelancers. If the articles don't have taglines at the end of articles, you can check the masthead (the list of editors, writers, etc.) at the front of the publication to see who is a staff writer and who isn't.

Don't worry if you start with only four or five magazines on your Heart List. The number will grow over time, and it will change as well. Some of the magazines will move from your Heart List to your Magazine Corral. These are the magazines with editors who have recognized your talent and who publish your articles on a regular basis. As your Magazine Corral grows, so will your career and your income. But your Heart List should never dwindle. As soon as you start writing for one publication, move it off of your Heart List and into your Magazine Corral. Then fill the vacant spot on your Heart List with at least one new magazine.

Below the corkboard of my Writer's Taffy Machine is a second corkboard divided roughly in half. On the left side is my corral, the fourteen or fifteen magazines I write for regularly. On the other side is my Heart List, currently with fifteen magazines. I keep these two lists on my wall to help me stay awake to this game of turning Heart List magazines into Corral magazines. Several of the magazines in my corral started on my Heart List, including *Modern Maturity, Boys Life, Vegetarian Times, Utne Reader,* and *Yoga Journal.*

I know it's only a matter of time before the other fifteen will move from the Heart List to the Corral. Why? Because I target my best ideas to them. I've even told editors when I call to get information about their magazine, "Your publication is on my Heart List, so you'll be hearing a lot from me." Most of them laugh, but I figure it's only fair to let them know they're about to be added to my Writers Corral. After all, if magazines can have stables of writers (and they do), why can't writers have a magazine corral?

Magazine Dissection

Once your Heart List is underway, your market research work is far from over. In fact, it's just begun. Now is the time to really dig into those magazines you're planning to write for and get to know them intimately. To facilitate this process, look at the Magazine Outline Form on the next pages.

MAGAZINE OUTLINE

Magazine _____ Editor
_____ Date_____

READER: M__ F__ B__, age range _____, Prof___
Bus ____ Fam ____
Special interests of readers

_____
_____
_____

Common interests

_____
_____
_____
_____

Income range _____ (look at people in
ads.)
     Description of typical reader

_____
_____

ISSUES OUTLINED: _____ ,_____
,_____

ARTICLE TYPES: (# OF EACH)
___/___/___ How-to___/___/___ Profile___/___/___
Humor___/___/___ Personal exp.___/___/___
Inspiration___/___/___ Self-help___/___/___
Travel___/___/___ Nostalgia___/___/___ H. interest

__/__/__ Opinion__/__/__
Expose__/__/__ Round-up__/__/__

ARTICLE TOPICS: (# OF EACH)
__/__/__ Travel__/__/__
Business__/__/__ Finance __/__/__
Relationship__/__/__ Sport__/__/__
Fit./health __/__/__ Nutrition__/__/__
Celebrity__/__/__ History
__/__/__ Beauty__/__/__ High
tech__/__/__ Building __/__/__
People__/__/__ Psychology__/__/__
Education __/__/__ Children__/__/__
Science__/__/__

ADVERTISERS: (PREDOMINANT PRODUCTS OR SERVICES)

_____

_____

ARTICLE FORMAT: (FEATURES)
Types of leads most common?

_____

_____

_____

Avg. # words _____. Quotes _____. Stats
_____ Style_____

Writing styles

_____

_____

35

DEPARTMENTS: (Names, topics, average word count)

This form can be useful in helping you keep track of the kinds of articles each magazine publishes. Use this as you study at least three recent back issues of a magazine.

If you don't subscribe to a magazine on your list, check the local library for copies. Some second-hand bookstores also carry recent back issues. If you can't locate copies, you can contact the magazine and find out what they charge for back issues. This isn't a place to scrimp. Pay the $10-$15 it might cost to get the back issues to study. Consider it part of the operating (and tax-deductible) expenses of being a writer. Here's why.

One of the top complaints magazine editors have about freelance writers is that they don't take the time to study the magazines that they query, and therefore, send story ideas that aren't applicable to those magazines. By studying the magazines carefully and systematically, you'll be head and shoulders above the crowd of other writers vying for the chance to publish and be paid for their writing. So, here's another big coaching tip:

STUDY THE MAGAZINES, starting with those on your Heart List.

Since I work well with structure and like using forms to help me learn, I use the Magazine Outline Form to aid me in the dissection process. The form is set up to assist me in my goal of getting a good overview of three back issues of a magazine. I start by determining the characteristics of the magazine's ideal reader. There are a couple of good ways to become acquainted with the average reader, your end customer.

First, read some of the letters to the editors. Almost every magazine has such a department. There you'll find real live readers sharing what they like and don't like about the magazine. It's a great way to not only become familiar with the readers but to also get some great ideas for future articles to pitch.

Second, look closely at the advertisements where you'll find a visual image of the magazine's reader. Since magazines operate from the advertising revenues they receive, advertisers invest a lot of money to target their ads to their audience. Also, reading the ads can often give you a look inside the psyches of the readers, since they're written to appeal to their wants, needs, and desires. Scanning the ads will give you a good idea of the readers' interests and, therefore, the types of articles the editorial department will be interested in receiving. But that doesn't mean that you should pitch articles about particular advertisers. Most magazines have strict demarcation lines between editorial and advertising.

Next look at the types of articles the magazine publishes. Using the outline form, count the number of different types of articles in the three back issues so you'll know the types to suggest to the editors. Do they use how-to articles, profiles, Q & A interviews, essays, personal experience pieces, or travel articles? It's far more likely the magazine will be interested in your "6 Nutritious Ways to Cook Chicken" if they run how-to articles and recipes. If they prefer personal experience pieces, you might want to slant your idea differently—how you sent your spouse to the hospital when you learned to cook chicken.

Combine the types of articles written with the predominant subjects they like to run and you'll be well on your way to hitting a home run with your queries.

Count up the different subjects they focus on until you see a pattern emerging. You'll know not to send a romance story to a magazine that doesn't take fiction, and you'll discover that you can suggest your "6 Nutritious Ways to Cook Chicken" because they run two to three nutrition pieces each issue.

Another area to focus on are the departments of the magazine. You can determine which articles are departments by looking at the table of contents. Typically, the department name will be listed, with the article title underneath. Department names remain the same month after month. This is often where a new freelance writer can break into a magazine, especially if the magazine is well known and the writer isn't. For instance, it's unlikely a magazine like *AARP Magazine* is going to offer a feature to a new writer, but they may give that same writer a chance on a departmental piece. Departmental pieces are usually short, so if the new freelance writer doesn't come through, either by missing the deadline or sending in an inferior piece, the magazine can fill the small gap of a 200- to 300-word departmental piece (sometimes known as a filler) much easier than chasm of a 3000-word feature.

Does this mean you should only develop and send in ideas that will fit in a department when you're trying to break into a new magazine? No. As with every rule, there are exceptions.

My first piece for *New Age Journal* and *Yoga Journal* were both feature articles; other times I've started writing for magazines such as *Boys' Life* and *Modern Maturity* at the departmental level. The point is to not overlook the departments as a great place to get acquainted with the editor and demonstrate your value as a dependable, gifted, freelancer.

Once you've gained a broad overview of the magazine, the next step is to take a close look at the articles — especially the types of articles you'd like to write. Let's say you want to write interviews and profiles, and you've found a magazine that takes these kinds of articles. Scan through the contents to see which ones you're naturally attracted to. Then sit back and start reading, but not in the same way you've read them before. Now, you must be more than a reader; you must also be a writer. It's helpful to have a pad and paper handy to take notes. Here are some of the questions to ask yourself as you read.

1. What kinds of leads are most often used in the magazine?
    a. Do they prefer running anecdotal leads?
    b. Leads with startling facts and figures?
    c. Leads that paint a picture?
    d. Others?

The ability to write a powerful, captivating lead is an important attribute of a successful writer. If you can't hook the reader (and the editor) in the first paragraph, the chances are good that they won't hang around to get to the good stuff later on. A reader will simply flip the page to the next article or put the magazine down. An editor is likely to toss your idea aside, and go on to the next writer's idea on the tall stack that covers her desk.

2. How long are the articles?
    a. Are the features in the 1,500-2,000 word range or do they run longer — 2,500 to 3,000 — or are they a mixture?
    b. How long are the departmental pieces?
    Of course, you don't have to count every word in the magazine. You can get a close enough estimate by counting the words in a column inch and then measuring the number of inches in an article. (Also, you can often determine the length a magazine is looking for from their writers' guidelines, which we'll study in more depth later.)

3. Is there a prevalent tone to the articles?
    a. Are most of them serious?
    b. Technical?
    c. Light and humorous?
    Of course, the tone will vary somewhat from article to article, but each magazine tends to have a particular voice. As a writer, you'll want to match that voice as closely as possible.

4. How do the articles end?
    Strong endings are almost as important as strong leads, so read over several endings to get a sense of how to write the types of endings the editor likes.

Other areas to look at in the magazine include the masthead and the bylines at the end of the articles.

You'll find the masthead at the front of the magazine, and it will give you some idea about the editorial department's structure and staff. The meaning of editorial titles can vary from magazine to magazine; one magazine will want the managing editor to receive your article idea, while another magazine may prefer that you direct it to a senior editor. Since magazine editors also tend to change jobs and publications frequently, don't depend on an old issue to give you the correct editor's name.

The best plan is to call ahead or check the Web site if you're in doubt.

Often, large magazines will have specialized editors listed on the masthead; for instance, an editor for food, one for travel, another for fiction, and so on. In these cases, it's easy to determine where you should send your ideas. (More on what form these ideas should take in a later chapter.)

Looking at the bylines, or the part of the magazine that profiles the contributors of the magazine, will help you determine how much or how little the magazine uses freelance writers. Today, with the rising cost of running a magazine, freelance writers are used quite often in most magazines. Still, some prefer to use only their staff writers — in which case, your submissions will not be welcome.

Again, if in doubt, call the magazine, and ask for someone in the editorial department. Once you reach the right department, ask if they accept freelance submissions. While you have them on the telephone, go ahead and ask them which areas are most open to new writers.

If you don't ask for a particular editor (and sometimes even when you do), you'll be directed to an editorial assistant. While editorial assistants are at the bottom of the pecking order, don't disregard them. Treat them with the respect and dignity they deserve. After all, you can use a friend at any level of the operation, and an editorial assistant may one day be the assistant editor or even move up to senior editor or higher. When treated with respect and common courtesy, I've found editorial assistants to be most helpful and quite willing to answer my questions.

Work That Pays

This market research is time-consuming. It can be hard work, too, for some writers. For others, it's fun scanning through magazines and learning what kinds of articles they like to run. In either case, it's work that will pay big dividends down the road. Take it from someone who had to learn the hard way.

At the start of my writing career, I was like many other writers, more interested in writing what I wanted to write than I was in finding out what magazines wanted to print. Even though I had other, more experienced writers urge me to conduct market research, it sounded like too much work to me. So, I would pick what I considered good ideas and I'd "shotgun" them out to 10 to 15 magazines. Some of the magazines I'd read, a few of them I might have studied, but for the most part they were simply names in a book, most from *The Writers' Market*.

Not surprisingly, most of the ideas resulted in my receiving an avalanche of form rejection letters. Once in awhile I'd score, but in the process, I wasted a lot of time and postage. Developing a Heart List and spending the time on market research has paid off with big dividends, and both need to be an active part of your work routine as a freelance journalist. In fact, I've found that most freelance writers who specialize in writing for magazines spend in the neighborhood of forty to sixty percent of their time in some form of marketing, whether it's studying magazines, writing new idea proposals, or networking. While your first love may be writing, your second love needs to become marketing and research if you want to be successful as a freelance journalist.

Here are some action steps that will move you down the path to finding your most likely markets.

Call to Action Assignment

1. On a pad of paper or in your notebook start a Heart List of the magazines where you would love to see your articles.

2. Start collecting new magazines to add to your list. Ask your friends for outdated magazines, search the grocery stores, newsstands, and bookstores for new markets for your ideas. Make another display on a corkboard for your Heart List and Magazine Corral.

3. Set a goal to spend some time each week studying and dissecting magazines from your Heart List, while also capturing new article ideas that come to mind as you read through the magazines. Add them to your Taffy Machine.

4. Begin linking your ideas with the magazines. Which ideas would fit which magazines?

Chapter 5 --
Fanning the Spark: Developing Ideas

If you've been following along with the exercises at the end of the chapters, you now have a list of possible article ideas. If you have a bountiful supply, your future as a writer is off to a healthy start. If not, your desire to be a writer could wither into a fantasy. Besides, collecting ideas is a lot of fun, especially when you realize that any one of them might end up producing a few hundred or even thousands of dollars.

How do you turn the raw material of an idea into a legitimate article? In this chapter, we'll look at how to develop an idea into not just one but possibly several good articles.

Picture in your mind, for a moment, a large juicy orange, just floating in space. Imagine a sharp knife cutting through the center of the orange. Now, let's put the two pieces back together, and take another slice at it, but this time we'll make a much smaller cut, not through the center but through a small portion of it, leaving one small piece and a second much larger piece.

As you can see, while it was the same orange, the two cuts produced orange slices that looked quite different. The same is true for ideas. Depending on how you slice them, you can develop vastly different story ideas. This is what is commonly called the slant of the story.

As Lisa Collier Cool writes in her book *How to Sell Every Magazine Article You Write*, the slant or angle of an idea is "what makes a submission right for one magazine, wrong for another." Having a well thought-out and defined slant will not only make your idea more appealing to the editor, it will also make the article easier to write. A common error of many aspiring writers is that their slant is much too broad to cover the idea thoroughly in a magazine article. Another fatal flaw is that the slant has been "written to death" by other writers and has no zip or pizzazz left in it.

Of course, if you have a fresh idea that no one else has covered yet, you may not need to worry much about the slant. Cool relates the story of offering a story idea on pheromones at a time when no one even knew how to pronounce the word, much less what it meant. So it was easy for her to sell the idea of writing about these natural chemicals that attract the sexes to each other.

Let's take a little closer look at how to develop a powerful slant that will result in an editor saying yes to your idea. Let's take something that everybody knows at least a little about and see how many different slants we can develop.

How about chocolate, the food of the gods? Well, right in that sentence you might have a good starting point. What makes chocolate such a popular confectionery? You could write an article for a scientific publication like *Discovery* that delved into the chemical make-up of chocolate and why so many people love its taste. Or you could write a humorous story about how your love for chocolate has gotten you into a heap of trouble your whole life. With just a little additional refinement you could send such an idea to several different magazines. Or, you can change the slant again to disclose how, as a man, chocolate has gotten you into a lot of trouble with women. How about the health benefits of chocolate? Of course, chocolate is mostly known for all the reasons it's not good for you, so an article on how it can improve your health could be a new twist on a popular subject and could be sold to a number of different magazines that either focus on health or have a health department.

To look just a little further, how about a 'how-to' article. It could be how to include chocolate in your holiday meals or six different ways to enhance your love life with chocolate. As you can see, the ideas are just about endless, and we've really just begun.

As you begin to develop your ideas into sharp, crisp, well-slanted article proposals, you'll want to start calling upon your market research information to help you develop slants that will be attractive to your Heart List magazines. For example, if I have an idea in my Taffy Machine to write something about the positive benefits of play, I could then look at my other board with my Heart List and Magazine Corral to see where I'd like to submit such an idea. Let's pick *Intuition Magazine*. Their tag line is "A Magazine for the Higher Potential of the Mind." Keeping that in mind, how about an article on how play can improve one's creativity? Of if the magazine is *Veterinary Economics*, the slant might be "Eight Ways to Lighten Up Your Practice," an article I wrote just recently.

Another fun approach to developing the right slant for an idea is to brainstorm as many ideas as you can come up with on a particular topic and then look to see which ones will fit the magazines on your Heart List. In this way, it's quite easy to develop several different article proposals from just one idea. This can be a sound way to leverage your efforts because you may be able to write two or more articles from the same research. Since research is a major investment of your time, you'll want to leverage it into as many assignments as possible.

To help me stay on track in developing ideas that would sell, I created an Article Development Form . I've refined it a bit over the years, and it's proven to be a very useful tool, so we'll use it now to develop an idea.

ARTICLE DEVELOPMENT FORM

BASIC IDEA: _____ DATE: _____

_____

_____

CAPSULE SENTENCE:_____

_____

_____

RESEARCH (INCLUDE SOURCES):_____

_____

_____

_____

_____

_____

POINT SYSTEM: ___ On Purpose (30) ___ Passion (30) ___
Marketability (20) ___ Profitability (20)
On back, answer following questions:
1- What leads does the editor like best?
2- How long are most of the leads?
3- What makes this story important?
4- What is the most interesting facet of the subject?

MAGAZINE   SLANTS

_____

                                  _____

_____

                                  _____

_____

                                  _____

_____

_____

                                           _____

_____

                                           _____

TEST QUESTIONS:

Do I really want to do this story?_____

Am I capable of doing this article? _____

How much would this article cost me?_____

What use would I have for this material if the editor

doesn't want it?_____

_____

Will there be a market for reprints?_____

Are there possible spin-off articles?_____

We'll start with a basic, unpolished, and unfocused idea. I'll pick one from my Taffy Machine board that comes from a book I recently received from a publicist. You remember that a publicist's job is to get his or her client's name into print, in a positive way, of course. This particular publicist, Anne Sellaro, initially contacted me about her client, Dr. Marti Becker, a veterinarian who has developed a special interest in the pet-family bond. He is also one of the editors of *Chicken Soup for the Pet Lovers' Soul*. As it turned out, Dr. Becker was not a fit for the article that Anne had in mind, but as we continued to talk, we discovered we shared many common interests besides pets and vets.

When I shared with her my "pet" project, Project Purpose, Anne began throwing names and stories out faster than I could keep up, and they were all connecting. She even threw out a name or two of people who weren't her clients yet but whose work she really believed in, a sure sign of a publicist who will go far in her field.

One of the ideas she gave me was about another client, John Perkins, who had written a book entitled *Shape Shifting: Shamanic Techniques for Global and Personal Transformation*. I was enthralled by Anne's commentary about John's life as he searched the globe for shamans whose wisdom he could then share with a world in much need of it. I trusted my writer's intuition to know that John's book and personal story would make one or more great articles.

I also knew that several of the different magazines in my corral would be interested.

So, with that background, let's develop this basic idea into one or more well-polished and publishable magazine articles, using the Article Development Form.

We'll start by giving the idea a name; let's use "Shape Shifting." The name merely gives the idea a tag. We'll use the name to start a file folder on the idea, as well as tracking the idea's progress through our Taffy Machine. The next step is to begin to sharpen the focus of the idea. We'll do this with a capsule sentence or two. Ideally we would like to be able to encapsulate our idea about shape shifting into one succinct statement, but this isn't always possible. However, we do want to carve out a small enough piece from this chunky idea that we can thoroughly cover it in 1500 -3000 words, the length of most features. If you can't capture the essence of the idea in one or two sentences, then you need to sharpen the focus some more.

With an idea as broad as "shape shifting and other shamanic techniques for global and personal transformation," we can easily carve out many great story ideas. Here are a few. Since I love writing profiles about people, I might start by encapsulating what a profile of John Perkins could cover. Something like this:

Former Peace Corp volunteer turned author, environmentalist and businessman John Perkins, the founder of Dream Change Coalition, is on a mission to collect shamanic wisdom from around the world and bring it back to modern civilization. Along the way to fulfilling his mission, Perkins has led an extraordinary life, as he has straddled two radically different realities.

As I reviewed this "straight off the top of my head" capsule statement, I find it might be a worthwhile lead for a query letter, perhaps even for the article, but it lacks a certain specificity to encapsulate what the article will be about. So, I work from there to see if I can bring in a tighter focus. One way to do this is to slant it for a particular kind of magazine. Obviously, if I'm interested in getting this story into a business magazine, the slant would be quite different than if I'm submitting it to a consciousness raising journal like *Intuition Magazine* or *Body and Soul*. Let's see if we can write two different capsule statements, one for each. First, for *Intuition Magazine*:

Former Peace Corp volunteer turned author, environmentalist and businessman John Perkins is on a mission to save the world by bringing back the ancient wisdom of shamans from many different cultures. Through decades of training with Amazonian and Andean shamans, Perkins has become a facilitator of their indigenous knowledge and offers this wisdom through his own workshops, escorting others to these far off homelands, and through other entrepreneurial ventures including Dream Change Coalition and POLE.

In looking over this revision, I see that while it's a bit longer than I'd ideally like to have as a capsule statement, it's more focused than the last one. Also, often profiles are, by their very nature of being an overview of someone's life, a bit broader in scope and therefore longer articles.

Let's see if we can create a sharper capsule statement for a piece that might appear in a business magazine or one of the in-flight magazines that often publish business-related articles:

Former Peace Corp volunteer John Perkins has made some radical changes in his life, from being a high level consultant to the U. N. to later successfully establishing his own environmentally friendly power company. Since selling the multi-million dollar enterprise, he has devoted his life to saving the rain forests by escorting influential Americans into the wilds of South America to study at the feet of native shamans and medicine men.

These capsule sentences can often be the jumping off point for the kind of lead to introduce the idea to editors. As we'll see later in the chapters about writing effective query or proposal letters, one effective format is to start the letter with a possible lead. This approach serves double or even triple duty. It introduces the idea to the editor in an engaging manner, while showing the editor that you can write an effective lead. You may also find the lead you write in the query letter becomes the lead for the article. (Frequently, though, by the time you've done the research, and started writing, an even better lead presents itself.)

Capsule sentences are a useful way to focus your idea into a workable length article and help you target the idea to a particular segment of the market. If, as in the case of the shape shifting idea, you'd like to develop the idea for several different types of magazines, spend the time to develop different slants, beginning with a variety of capsule sentences.

By now, you may be wondering where the information comes from for your capsule sentence. It often comes from the source of the original idea, or from some additional research you've done. The particular content for the John Perkins idea came from the background information provided by his publicist, one of the reasons I love working with publicists in this way.

As you continue to develop yourself as a freelance writer, you'll find that the process of developing capsule sentences will also spur your imagination to come up with likely magazines for each different slant. Jot these magazines down next to each slant, then expand the list from your growing database of magazines and other writing outlets like Web sites.

Weighing The Options With A Point System

When you have lots of ideas flowing into your Taffy Machine, you can be selective about which ones you actually decide to devote your time and energy to developing and writing. Some ideas look good on the surface but simply don't stand up to close scrutiny.

On the Article Development Form I've included two areas that help me decide which articles to pursue and which to either put on the back burner for later or discard altogether. These two areas are the Point System and the Idea Test Questions.

Let's look at the Point System first. I score four areas to help me decide if the idea I'm developing is really one for me. These four areas may not be the ones you use for yourself, or you may decide to change the weight each one carries. That's up to you. I score myself heavily on the side of passion and purpose. When I take on an idea, I'll have a lot more fun, write much more effectively, and will probably make more money if I'm working on ideas that really interest me. So, I score a total of sixty percentage points in the areas of "On Purpose" and "Passion."

On Purpose means that the idea is right up my alley. It's the type of material I love to write about, it's consistent with my writing goals, and it's likely to forward my career, at least a little bit. Passion is my interest measure. The idea may not be something I know a lot about, but it's something I'd like to know in more depth. That's the case with the John Perkins idea. I don't know a lot about shamanism, although I'm fascinated by the subject. I also have a strong desire to travel to the rain forests someday. It's high on the Passion scale.

Since the article ideas I'm developing would likely be profiles and/or interviews, this idea also ranks high on the On Purpose scale. The articles would fall under Project Purpose and could open new markets for these types of articles. So, the John Perkins idea ranks high on the On Purpose scale as well.

It also ranks well in the third area, Marketability. There are at least four or five major ways to slice the idea into different slants and different markets. This means that, with very little extra work, I could send proposals out to dozens of magazines. And since most of the magazines I have in mind are major periodicals, the ideas rank high in the last category, Profitability. In other words, the John Perkins idea is a clear winner in my book.

Other ideas don't always fare so well. The business stories for *US Air Magazine* wouldn't have passed the Point System test if I had used it in those days. They would have been high on the Profitability scale since the magazine pays well, and they were certainly marketable since the editor was assigning them to me. But for the On Purpose and Passion scales, they bottom out.

If I'm in doubt about a story idea I use the second test to help me decide. The Idea Test Questions also help me look at the whole picture and not get too carried away with my passion for certain subjects. Let's look at each question:

1. Do I really want to do this story?

This question is to remind me to stop for a moment to examine how much the story turns me on. Occasionally when I do this I realize that I've stumbled upon a great idea that "should" be written. For example, recently my wife and I have gone through a series of tax audits. During the process I had the notion that an article on how to survive a tax audit or how to make friends with your tax auditor would make for an interesting article, but when I stopped and asked this question, I realized it wasn't an article for me. The second question helped as well.

2. Am I capable of doing this article?

Often I get an idea to write an article that simply isn't one that I'm capable of doing well. The tax audit idea fell in this area, especially when I looked at all the technical information that might have to be included. The truth is, I'm not an accountant or tax attorney, and although I could certainly find competent experts who could answer my questions, in the final analysis, I'd find such interviews boring.

3. How much would this article cost me?

Some ideas are simply too expensive to pursue, or they have a high risk factor involved. Cost may be monetary in nature, or it may be time or other factors. An expose on the Mafia could make for fascinating reading, but the amount of danger it could put me in might make the cost too high. With the John Perkins piece, if I were to write it as a personal account of my travels with John to the wilds of the Amazon, I'd need to either get several assignments or one magazine to pay the travel expenses for me to be able to pursue the story. If the other factors weren't so strong, I might have decided not to pursue the story, but for the chance to cover a story in the rain forests of South America, I figured it's worth the risk. Plus, I realize that, while my first choice would be to cover the story in person, I also knew I could do a credible job simply profiling John. This is actually what happened. Months after I sent a query out on this idea to *Intuition Magazine*, I received a call from the editor. The query had languished in her "to be read" stack for most of that time. That's my fault because I failed to follow up as well as I could. But now, suddenly, there was a deadline looming and the editor needed a hot story fast. Could I do it? "You bet," I answered.

Less than a month later, the final product was in her hands.

4. What use would I have for this material if the editor doesn't want it?

Sometimes you spend hours and hours working on a story just to have it killed. Painful but true. In those cases, it's useful to have already considered this question. If the story is so specialized that only one or two magazines might want it, or if it's on a topic that has a limited time span of interest, it could be a high-risk idea to pursue. Luckily, I've only had a few articles killed, but it's happened. But by having asked this question I've been able to place the killed stories elsewhere, sometimes for more money than the previous contract, and usually without needing to change anything. Go figure. To me, it says that even when an article is killed, it may not be because there's anything wrong with the article. It simply may not be a fit for that particular magazine or editor. This is another great place to follow your writer's instincts. If you feel the article is good, shop it around as it is. You may be pleasantly surprised at the outcome.

For example, I wrote a Q & A style interview of Bo Lozoff for a magazine that I'd queried. While they loved the idea and gave me the go ahead, they weren't pleased with the finished product, and asked me to go back and ask several other questions – questions that I felt were overly intrusive and argumentative, but at first, I decided to give it a shot. Ten minutes into the follow up interview, I knew I should have trusted my initial instincts. I apologized to Bo and told him I'd get back to him if I needed anything else. I then contacted the editor and took the kill fee.

I then took the original article and offered it to another publication – one with much more prestige. They jumped on it, and offered to pay me substantially more than the original publication. Boy, was I a happy camper. I had maintained my writer's integrity, and earned not only the kill fee from the original publication but a second fee along with a prestigious clip to use in the future.

I wish I could say following my instincts always pays off this way, but unfortunately, it's not always the case. It does happen often enough, however, for me to know that it pays in the long run to trust myself.

5. Will there be a market for reprints?
Some articles have a broad appeal, making it possible to sell them multiple times, while others are destined for a one-shot appearance. Asking this question in the early stage of developing an idea helps me stay on the outlook for different places I can sell it in the future. I've sold some of my articles four or five times.

Recently, I've developed a "recycling project" for my Project Purpose articles, after realizing that most of the reprinted articles were sold to editors who found me in some way rather than my seeking them out. Just as most auto dealerships have a used or "previously owned" lot next to their new cars, there can be lot of good mileage in an article that's been published just once.

61

One of the hallmarks of successful freelancers is that they are always looking for ways to leverage their time and talent. Recycling articles is one of those ways.

6. Are there possible spin-off articles?

Re-slanting an article is another great way to leverage the work of developing an idea. Like question 5, this question is useful to ask early, not only to help you decide whether to pursue the idea further, but also to help you start looking for ways to re-slant it. For example, when you get the first assignment and start interviewing people, it's possible to ask additional questions that might not be pertinent to the original slant but will come in handy when you re-slant the story to other magazines.

It's easier to re-slant an article if you plan to do it before getting too far into the development process. However, it's possible to back into it as well. In this case, it may be necessary to call your experts back to ask a few new questions or to search out one or two new resources. Most of this extra legwork can be avoided by knowing at the beginning of the project that you're working on more than one article.

None of these questions has a right or wrong answer. They are simply useful to help you look carefully at what ideas you want to pursue. After all, you'll spend a significant amount of time on the many ideas that you take all the way through your Taffy Machine. The Point System and the Idea Test Questions will help you reduce the number of ideas that get rejected at the end of the process.

Call to Action Assignment

1. Pick at least three of your hottest ideas, the ones you would really like to write about and that seem to have several likely markets. Write the basic idea on a sheet of paper or use the Article Development Form.

2. Develop these ideas thoroughly. See how many different slants or spins you can create with each idea.

Chapter 6
How to Sell Every Article You Write

Sell every article you write. Does that sound too good to be true? Well, it's not. The way to sell every article you write is to sell it before writing it. Why spend hours researching, writing, editing, and revising just to find out no one wants an article on the mating habits of your daughter's guinea pig?

The key to streamlining your work so you're spending time on the ideas you're most passionate about and getting paid for each article is to develop the skill of writing effective query letters. But what is a query letter, exactly? Answering that question is what this chapter is about.

A query letter is a sales letter. For a query letter to be effective, you must sell the editor on two important things — your article idea, and yourself as the writer of choice for writing the piece. Fail at either one, and you'll be the proud recipient of another letter — the infamous rejection letter. Of course, you can be successful in selling an editor on your idea and yourself and still receive a rejection for many different reasons that we'll explore later, but you'll significantly increase your sales to magazines by developing the fine art and science of writing effective, attention-grabbing, query letters.

Attention-Grabbing Queries

The best way I know to help writers learn how to write effective query letters is to look at some that have resulted in contracts for articles. These are actual query letters that I've written that resulted in sales. I'll also point out some mistakes I made in these letters so perhaps you can learn from my mistakes rather than make the same ones yourself. It will also illustrate that you can make a mistake a two, or three, or many along the way (but not all in the same letter) and still be successful. Let's look at the first example, a query that landed me my first assignment for *Omni Magazine*. (See Query Letter Appendix)

Omni Magazine was one of the first magazines that moved from my Heart List to my Corral. Being a science enthusiast and science fiction buff at heart, I'd been reading *Omni* for years, so it was a natural for my list. At the same time, writing for them in 1992 appeared, at the time, to be quite a stretch for me. Still, I figured why not aim high with at least some of the magazines on my Heart List. The idea paid off with *Omni*.

(NOTE: Unfortunately, a few years after I began writing for *Omni* they moved from a print format to one of the first magazines to appear solely on the Internet. My writing for them had nothing to do with them going out of print. Promise.)

The idea for the query that sold came from a short article I read in my local newspaper on two scientific breakthroughs with the tobacco plant. In fact, most of the facts and information in the query came from the newspaper article. Of course, after receiving the assignment, I did my own research for the information that appeared in the *Omni* piece.

Let's look at this first example from start to finish to see what works about it and one or two items that I would change today. First, the letterhead is simple and uncomplicated. One of the first actions I took after launching my full- time freelance writing career was to go out and order nice stationery with a simple, business style letterhead. As I remember it, 500 sheets cost around $300. Unfortunately, well before I had used it all, I moved to a new address. I then realized that I didn't need such extravagant supplies. Today I use two or three different letterheads, depending on whether I am presenting myself as a doctor of veterinary medicine or as the director of Life On Purpose. They're set up in my computer as blank templates. I have a selection of nice paper upon which I print the letter and letterhead. This approach is less expensive and much more flexible. If anything changes on my letterhead, it's a simple typing change that costs nothing.

The format of this query letter is one of my favorites. After the address and salutation, I start right off with a working title and a possible lead. By the way, one thing I'd change about this letter is that since I didn't know the editor well when I wrote this query, I'd start with "Dear Ms. Murphy," rather than "Dear Erin." I would reserve the more informal salutation for later, after I had spoken to her on the phone and we had become acquainted.

Starting a query letter with a sample lead is effective for several reasons. First, it gives you an opportunity to show the editor that you can write an effective, engaging lead, something that's important to editors. It also carries you right into the idea, just as a lead should in an article. Third, it's visually appealing, especially when the lead is set off a bit from the rest of the letter with the different size font and indentation.

Why is this important? Well, imagine what it's like to be an editor for a moment. It's likely that you work for a magazine that's under-staffed, because just about every magazine has far more work than they have people to do the work. So, you have many different responsibilities, including reading the hundreds or thousands of query letters that flood into your office every week. But that's not all you do. You're probably also editing a number of articles for an upcoming issue, as well as writing an article or two yourself. Of course, there are also the endless number of editorial meetings to attend, plus managing the assistant editor who's just come on board and who knows nothing about what's going on. Not to mention that the executive editor and publisher have been hinting about completely redesigning the magazine, and you can't help but wonder if that might mean your job may be redesigned away. You get the idea?

Meanwhile, there are all those writers out there who keep pestering you with their letters and phone calls. Of course, at one level you realize you need those writers – well, at least some of them. They're the lifeblood of the editorial content of the magazine, but couldn't just a few thousand of them take a break every now and then so you can catch up with the slush pile of unsolicited manuscripts and queries?

In short, many editors do not come to the stack of query letters with excitement and anticipation. They're mostly interested in cutting the stack down to size as quickly as possible so they can get on with the dozen or so other duties that they're behind on, while at the same time not missing the one or two great story ideas that might be lurking like diamonds among the mountain of slush.

So, your job as a writer is to make your letter stand out in a positive way. Now, there are many ways to make a letter stand out. Unfortunately, many of them will have it stand out in a negative way, which won't help you get an assignment. Here are some of the ways to have your letters stand out that you want to **avoid**:

- Using bright pink or multi-colored stationery more appropriate for your Aunt Milley's letters, or adding just a touch of your favorite perfume to the edges.

- Using so many different fonts and sizes that the letter looks like an anonymous note from a serial killer.

- Including catchy little trinkets like a refrigerator magnet with your name and phone number, or a pressed flower because, after all, your idea is "One Hundred Different Ways to Use Pressed Flowers." (Okay, maybe this last one could work).

Remember this one basic principle:

Your job as a freelance writer is to make the editor's job easier.

How can you do this with your query letters? One way is to make them visibly appealing while not stepping over the invisible boundary of being garish or too cute.

Breaking up your sentences into shorter paragraphs makes the reading easier on the eyes.

Setting off a sample lead so it looks like it will appear in the magazine works. And if you look down the page a little further you'll notice another eye-catching trick—bullets. Bullets break the page up into small, digestible chunks. If an editor is in a hurry, (which they almost always are), then he or she can quickly look over the lead, and then the bulleted points, to see if the query should be saved.

And, of course, the best way to catch an editor's attention is to write powerful and captivating material that will demonstrate your gift as a writer.

Now that we've covered the formatting of the letter, let's look at what should be in the content. Again, a sample lead can be very effective, but as we'll see in another example, it's not always necessary. I use this approach in probably seventy five percent of my query letters, but if I can't seem to come up with a catchy lead, I'll use another approach.

The next piece to include in your letter is some type of capsule sentence or paragraph. In this first example, the sentence reads, "This could be the lead for my article on the breakthrough research being conducted to transform tobacco from mass murderer to savior." The next step is to include the main points you plan to cover in the story, usually no more than four or five. If possible, you want these points to be filled with meaty facts and figures. After all, this is non-fiction we're writing. This will show the editor that you've done, at least, some preliminary research, a point definitely in your favor.

For the same reason, it's also a good idea to include who your sources for the story will be, as many as you know at this point. In the case of the tobacco story, the newspaper clipping gave me two experts, so I listed them in my letter.

One popular question I get from aspiring writers is if I contact the experts before I send in a query letter to be sure they are available and willing to be interviewed. The answer is, almost never. The exception to this would be if I'm interviewing a well-known person, such as a movie star or politician. Obtaining an interview with a celebrity can be more difficult. Most experts, like the ones listed in this example, are only too happy to talk to your about their work. In fact, if there's a problem, it's getting them to shut up! Often, experts will stray off the subject or will go into such details that they will lose you. I've had to learn when to interrupt someone who's going too far a field, and when to let them run with an idea.

Up to this point, everything we've included in the letter is designed to sell the editor on the idea. If you've done this well, there's only one step left -- being sure the editor gives the assignment to you.

Putting your Best Foot Forward

Selling yourself is often the most difficult part of writing a query letter because most of us have been taught from early childhood not to brag on ourselves. But, in a query letter, if you don't brag on yourself, nobody else will, and the editor is likely to just toss the idea aside or assign it to someone else.

But that's not fair, you may be saying. Well, it may not be fair but it's legal, since ideas cannot be trademarked or copyrighted. Products can be trademarked, and articles can be copyrighted, but not ideas.

So, it's important to learn the craft of putting your best foot forward. It may feel awkward to talk about yourself and your qualifications, especially if you don't have many or any publishing credits. This is where practice and creativity come in. For me, the difference between putting your best foot forward and bragging is that you're always careful to tell the truth when you put your best foot forward. Remember, part of your job as a writer is to learn how to shape a person's reality through the use of words. Perception is everything.

Of course, if your perception is that you aren't the perfect writer for the job, then you'll have difficulties also. Low self-esteem is a common affliction for writers. If this is the case for you, now is the time to start resolving those issues in whatever way you choose. In the meantime, fake it! That doesn't mean lie. Begin to practice writing those one to two paragraphs about yourself, making every word count to put your best foot forward. It's a little bit like going on a first date. You don't hang out your dirty laundry to someone you've just met, unless you're trying to get rid of them.

Let's look at the *Omni* letter again to see more clearly what I mean. I wrote:

"As a freelance writer with a strong science and medical background (see enclosed resume or biography), I'll successfully translate the technical jargon of the research into the language of the layman. "

I didn't say what my strong science and medical background was in the letter because I didn't feel it was necessary to do so. After all, my science background is primarily in biology and veterinary science, not botany or plant science. However, at the same time, I didn't lie. I do have a strong science and medical background, something an editor of *Omni Magazine* would find appealing in a freelance writer.

I also included some of the magazines for which I'd written, leading with the best known and most prestigious. Let's look at this a little more closely to see what I mean about putting your best foot forward without lying. At the time I wrote this letter, I'd had only one short piece appear in *Entrepreneur* , but would it have been to my advantage to say that? Of course not? Sometimes putting your best foot forward means <u>not</u> going into all the details.

This brings up one big error in this letter that I would never do today, but that I did in 1992. Luckily, I got away with it then. It's in the last paragraph:

"Since this would be the first time I've had the pleasure to write for Omni , I would be happy to write this article on speculation. "

Ouch! It pains me to read that sentence. What it says loud and clear to an editor is, "rank amateur, not a professional writer." Professional writers don't write on speculation. Writing on spec means you're agreeing to do all the research, writing and rewriting, on the hope the magazine will like it and buy it. It lets the magazine off the hook regarding any commitment to work with you on the piece.

After doing such a good job throughout the letter to present myself as a professional writer, I nearly blew it at the end. Luckily, the editor was willing to overlook the error. I received the assignment, which included a written contract to write the piece and NOT on speculation.

The Art Of Writing Query Letters

In the appendix of this book, I've included an assortment of query letters that have produced results for me, along with the beginnings of the articles that I wrote after getting the assignment. I recommend you study these examples before starting to write your own queries.

We'll now touch upon a few other fine points on how to write a query letter that will turn that spark of an idea you began with into moneymaking magazine articles that make a difference.

There are at least three different formats that I use for query letters. Using a lead at the beginning is my favorite, in large part because it's the style that has produced the best results. I like going with a winner. A slight modification of this can be seen in the example in the appendix -- *A One Woman Canine Crusade*.

This query also demonstrates that a query letter doesn't have to be long. This one is just over half a page, and yet it produced a nice assignment for me. In fact, I've written at least three articles about Chitra Besbroda, the one-woman crusader, for non-competing magazines.

You'll notice that there's no address or salutation at the beginning of this one. I use this format when submitting multiple queries to a magazine. I start with a regular query letter similar to our first example, and somewhere, either at the beginning or towards the end of it, I mention I'm sending more than one idea.

I've heard other successful writers who recommend sending only one article idea at a time. After all, why compete with yourself, they argue. Well, I'd much rather compete with myself than with other writers. I'd rather give an editor the dilemma of trying to decide which of my ideas to assign first, than have them decide to move right along to the next writer's query letter.

I've had good luck with multiple queries. More than once I've had editors give me multiple assignments. The best example of this was when I started writing for *Aspire*. I found out about them through an online forum for journalists, and contacted them through email. I sent them three different ideas, and they bought all three. I admit my timing was very good. For starters, *Aspire* was in the process of expanding from six issues a year to twelve, so they needed a lot more material. Secondly, they had just killed an article they'd been planning to run and needed to fill the slot quickly. One of mine fit the bill. But I wouldn't have had those types of results if I hadn't taken the initiative and sent them several ideas.

Now, let's look at the section of this query in which I put my best foot forward. In this example, I use what I call "straight talk" to make my point. "If you're looking for a non-partial report on this story, I'm not the writer to cover it." This brazen statement is intended to grab the editor's attention. Once I have her attention, I then go on to explain why I am the writer for the piece. I then end the letter with a simple, "Interested?" If so, the editor knows where to reach me. She was.

The third format I use for query letters is shown in the example, *Untroubled Youth,*, which you'll also find in the appendix. Notice, this one has no lead at the beginning of the letter. Why? Probably because, on that particular day, I couldn't come up with one I felt was strong enough. Although I don't write a sample lead, I do open the letter with some meaty facts to draw the editor into the idea. I'm proposing a profile about a young man who's had an amazing life in just his first twenty-two years, so I point out some of the highlights of his life:

- Peace marcher at age seven,
- Marathoner and business owner at ten, and
- Two-time representative of our country in Moscow before he'd turned sixteen.

This is a son any dad would be proud of. Of course, the fact that the dad I'm referring to is a well-known author and activist himself, John Robbins, doesn't hurt my point.

The whole first half of the letter is building a case for why this young man deserves to be profiled, by pointing out some of his unique qualities. Only then do I offer the slant that I'm proposing, the contrast between his life and many others of his generation. I then offer some of the key points I plan to cover in the piece.

Once again, I've spent most of my time selling the idea, before giving myself one short paragraph to sell myself. By the time this proposal was written, I'd formulated Project Purpose and started the Life On Purpose organization, so of course, I use this information to present myself with my best foot forward.

Practicing Putting Your Best Foot Forward

Here's a simple and fun exercise that will give you an opportunity to practice putting your best foot forward. For this exercise, you'll need a partner. If possible, use someone else who could benefit from the exercise, either as a writer or in some other capacity. Otherwise, just use a supportive friend or spouse.

First, decide who will be "A" and who will be "B." If the other person isn't interested in practicing putting their best foot forward but is only helping your out, then you be "A" and only go through the exercise once.

In the first part of the exercise, the "A" person will have two minutes to introduce themselves to "B." It doesn't really matter that the person may already have known you for years because you'll be introducing yourself differently. You'll be putting your best foot forward. In other words, it will sound like you're bragging on yourself, but remember, only say what is true; no lying. At the same time, it's good to stretch yourself a bit. Really lay it on thick. If you were in the top ten percent in your high school or college, say it. If you've raised three wonderful kids and they have gone on to live accomplished lives, take full credit for it. If you've been a hobbyist at something for fifteen years, include that as well. Say as many good things about yourself as you can think of in two minutes. Take a couple of minutes now to think about what you'll say, but don't limit yourself just to what you know to say now. Most people can get on a real roll with this exercise.

Now, here are "B's" instructions on how to listen. This exercise serves double duty. You'll be practicing putting your best foot forward and becoming a bit more comfortable with the notion. Meanwhile, your partner will be listening for topics and ideas that you could write about. It's fine if they want to jot down a few notes as you're introducing yourself.

At the end of the two minute introduction, "B" will then take a couple of minutes to tell you all the ideas for articles he heard from your introduction. Your job is to write them all down. Don't worry at this point if you don't think you could write on such subjects. Don't even worry if some of the ideas don't sound like they'd be much fun to write. This is all brainstorming. You can pick and choose from the list later.

After writing the list, if your partner is willing, switch roles and have him introduce himself as you listen for ideas. If he's interested in practicing putting his best foot forward, listen for ideas that would fit his interests. At the end, spend a couple of minutes debriefing the exercise with each other. What did you learn from the exercise? Were there things about the other person that you didn't know that surprised you? Did you say things about yourself that were

77

unexpected as well? What was the best idea that came from the exercise?

There's one last topic to cover about query letters -- clips. A clip is a sample of your work, an article that you've previously written for another publication that you can include in your query letter. A common question from new writers is, "What if I don't have any clips to send?" Well, then you can't send one, right? What some aspiring writers don't realize is, if you don't have any clips it's also not a good idea to mention anything about them. There are many different reasons a writer might not send a clip. You might have simply forgotten, perhaps the clips you have don't fit the particular subject or magazine you're sending the query to, perhaps you're such an experienced writer you just chose not to use clips. Whatever the reason, it's not in your best interest to point out to the editor that you're not sending clips because you don't have them.

But what about clips of articles from a local newspaper or small regional publication? If you have them, should you include them? This isn't quite so simple to answer because it will vary with each situation. Here's the place to look to decide whether to add a clip or not. Place yourself in the editor's shoes for a moment and ask the question, "Will sending this material strengthen my chances of getting the new assignment or weaken it?" If in doubt, I'd leave the clip out.

Even though I now have a filing cabinet full of sample articles I've written, if I don't have one that's a good match for the particular idea I'm marketing, I don't enclose a clip. I want everything that's included in a query letter to be in my favor. If it's not, or if I'm not sure it will be, I leave it out.

Call to Action Assignment

Ok, it's time for you to take at least one of your juiciest ideas that you've been developing and turn it into your first query letter. It helps to have one or more magazines in mind so you can customize the query to the magazine.

Coaching Tip: There are two important parts of the writing process -- the creative act of writing and the polishing process of editing. It's also important to not try to do both of these at the same time. It's a little like trying to drive a car with one foot on the accelerator and the other on the brake. It's rough on a car's engine and trying to write and edit at the same time is rough on a writer.

Your initial goal is to simply finish a 'rough' draft of the query letter. Then, put it away for a day or so, then with your editor hat on, go back and begin to polish it to perfection.

Chapter 7
Yes, No, and Handling
the Big R (Rejection)

If you follow the systematic approach we've outlined thus far, it's just a matter of perseverance and time before you'll receive a positive response to one of your queries. Of course, along the way you'll receive a significant number of rejection letters, or even worse, no response at all. So, before we jump to how to handle the good news of an acceptance, let's take a closer look at the more common occurrence — rejection.

Many people have a tremendous amount of baggage when it comes to one of the smallest words in the English language — no. It's mostly a learned behavior. As I've watched my daughter growing up, the first few years she didn't seem to have any problems with rejection. For example, while learning to walk, gravity rejected her countless times. She'd pull herself up on her pudgy, wobbly legs, stand there for a few seconds, then try letting go. As soon as she did, gravity rejected her attempts to stand and plop, down she'd go. She'd sit there for a few moments, then giggle and start all over.

Not so with many writers. In fact, I've talked to quite a few writers who have so much fear of being rejected that they won't even submit their material. That's one way to avoid rejection. It's just not a productive way to build a writing career. Let's look at how to deal with rejection in a more positive manner.

How about turning it in your favor? Here's how I went about doing just that. When I decided to try my hand at writing and getting published, I created a writing game. I call it the Big R Game. The rules are simple; in fact, there's only one, and it's summarized in the object of the game:

> **Collect as many rejections as you can as fast as you can while writing as well as you can.**

I set my target for 100. Now, I know this might sound a little crazy. Why would I set collecting rejections as one of my writing goals? Isn't that what a writer wants to avoid? Well, maybe in a perfect world, but the writing and publishing world isn't quite perfect. My rationale for starting such a game was simple. I knew that if I won at this game I'd be doing at least two things right: I'd be writing a lot and I'd be submitting what I wrote. These are the two most important activities a writer needs to do religiously and consistently if he wants to succeed at the larger game of being a published and profitable writer.

Playing the Big R Game also took the edge off of receiving those rejection letters. Each time I'd get one in the mail, I knew I was winning the game, not only the Big R game but also the much larger game of becoming successful as a writer. I viewed each rejection as one step closer to learning my craft. If you have a problem with rejection, try a few rounds of Big R. You may find it will lift your spirit and dissolve a lot of the resistance you've added to writing.

The other big benefit of the game is that if you set out to collect one hundred rejections, you're also going to get a fair amount of acceptances, which, for the purposes of the game would be failures, but what a great way to fail!

Dialing For Dollars

There's another step between sending out well-focused, timely ideas in the form of query letters and receiving assignments and rejection letters. It's one of the steps that most writers are terrible at. In fact, I've talked to a lot of experienced freelancers who cringe at even the idea of taking this step. It's getting on the phone and following up when you haven't heard from an editor within a reasonable amount of time.

Yes, despite what a lot of writers think, editors can be reached by phone and most of them are fairly adept at talking on the phone. In fact, the telephone can be one of your most powerful tools for generating business, in part because so many other writers are reluctant to do follow up calls. Here's how to go about it.

Keeping Track Of Time

To have your writer's taffy machine start churning out a regular supply of writing assignments, you want to keep the raw material flowing through it. Don't write a query or two, then sit at the mail box waiting for a reply. Keep gathering ideas, developing them, shaping them into queries, and sending them out. If you do, it won't be long before you'll be getting responses. At the same time, there will be some ideas that seem to get stuck in the gears of your machine.

These are the ones you want to follow up with a telephone call.

After mailing a query, take the card that you're using to keep track of the idea on your Writer's Taffy Machine and write the date the query was mailed. Next to it, write the date when you should receive a reply. This date will vary somewhat from magazine to magazine, so check the magazine's guidelines or *Writer's Market* to find out what the average turnaround time is. For most magazines it's between two and three months.

Then periodically, scan the board to see which magazines you haven't heard from. Pull those ideas off the board and start dialing for dollars. Here's how the conversation might sound once you reach the right editor:

"Hello, this is Brad Swift, I'm a freelance writer from North Carolina. I sent you a query on an idea, 'Shapeshifting in the New Millenium,' a profile of John Perkins of Dream Change Coalition. I mailed it out on August 23. Since I hadn't heard anything in over eight weeks, I thought I'd follow up to see if it fits your editorial needs at this time. When I first learned about Perkins I thought his story would be a perfect fit for your magazine."

Don't be surprised if the editor hasn't got a clue what you're talking about. After all, your query is one of hundreds that have come across her desk in the last eight weeks. But also, don't be put off by it if she isn't familiar with it. Simply continue:

"I understand if you can't recall it off the top of your head. Here's what the query is about: I'm suggesting a profile of John Perkins, a former Peace

Corp volunteer turned author, environmentalist, and businessman. Perkins, the founder of Dream Change Coalition, is on a mission to collect shamanic wisdom from around the world and bring it back to modern civilization. Along the way to fulfilling his mission, Perkins has led an extraordinary live as he has straddled two radically different realities."

Keep the description short, to the point, and as engaging as you can. This has two purposes. One, it might spur the editor's memory. Second, and more importantly, it may pique her curiosity. Then end your spiel with a suggestion:

"Would you like me to fax or email you a copy of the query so you won't have to search through your stacks of mail?"

If the editor says yes to this idea, and they often do, you've just moved your query out of the slush pile onto the top of the editor's desk. But don't stop there. Keep making it easy for the editor to work with you.

"I'll follow up in a few days to see whether you like my idea as much as I think you will. Should I call you back by the end of this week or next week?"

Whichever day you set up to follow up, be sure you do it. Depending on the editor's schedule, she may or may not have had a chance to review your material. If not, keep being of service and keep offering to follow up.

One reason I think follow-up calls are so important is that once you've spoken directly to an editor you stop being just a piece of paper among stacks of paper and you become a real person. And if you conduct yourself in a friendly, professional manner, the editor will likely realize that you're a person she can work well with, maybe not for the idea you sent, but maybe on some other idea down the road.

Follow-up calls are one of the most important opportunities you've got to build rapport and a relationship with a new editor. Leverage those calls in this way and a lot of those ideas that started out stuck in the taffy machine could turn into some of the most delectable assignments down the line.

Call to Action Assignment

Have fun with this assignment that will strengthen your ability to withstand rejection. Set a goal this week to make as many requests as necessary until you receive at least five 'nos.' The object of this game is to collect no's so feel free to swing out and make some outrageous requests. There's just one more rule to this game. Only make requests that you're willing to have accepted. In other words, don't ask someone to take you to Jamaica if you aren't willing to go with that person.

Chapter 8
Delivering the Goods

At this point you may be asking yourself, "But what do I do once I finally get an assignment?" I promise you, if you keep your Writer's Taffy Machine working, it's bound to happen sooner or later. In fact, with the Writer's Taffy Machine, it's likely to be sooner than later.

Before we move on to the next part of the Taffy Machine, there's one step that's not included. The very first thing to do once you have an assignment is to CELEBRATE!

Celebrate the accomplishment each and every time. Take a moment after you receive each assignment to acknowledge yourself for the great job you've done persevering. This will help you stay fresh and in touch with your passion for writing.

While the emphasis of the From Spark to Flame process and this book is marketing and all the steps that lead to assignments, I do want cover some of the basics of the actual process of writing the articles, along with some ideas that might not be so basic, but that I've found important to remember.

Clarity & Co-creativity

After the celebration is over, it's now time to get down to work and produce a great article that your editor will be pleased to pay you good money for. This next stage begins with clarity and co-creativity. In other words, you want to become as clear as possible what the editor is looking for from you and to come as close to delivering that as possible. Since clarity is the first stage of creativity, here are some of the things you want to know that will bring clarity to the assignment.

1.   How long will the article be? What is the word count?
2.   What kind of article will it be and where will it appear in the magazine? Will it be a departmental piece or a feature? Will it be an essay, a how-to, a profile, or a travel piece?
3.   What is the tone that the editor is looking for? Informative? Humorous? Serious? Satirical?
4.   Are there particular people that the editor wants to be sure you interview for the background information? If so, who are they?
5.   What is your timeframe for submitting the piece and in what form does the editor want it delivered?

The mindset that I've found to be most useful at this point is one of cooperation, collaboration and co-creativity. In other words, the editor and I are now engaged in a process of creating the best article possible. Ideally, I love talking with the editor over the phone with the intention of the call to be to gain as much clarity as possible as to how the editor envision the final piece to be. The clearer you are at the start, the less work you'll have at the other end in the form of rewrites.

It's been my experience that most editors enjoy working closely with their writers, even though their time is often filled with many other activities as well. Remember, your mantra: "How can I make my editor's job easier?" Keeping that in your sight while checking your ego at the door will pay off in big dividends including additional future assignments.

Contracts and Agreements

A common question I receive from new writers is, "Do I need a written contract or agreement?" My preference is yes, for one main reason. One, it helps provide clarity around what the two parties are agreeing to, and avoids sticky misunderstandings later. You might be surprised to find that although you're offering one time North American rights, which mean you're giving the magazine permission to publish the article one time in their North American publication, they may be expecting all rights in all different forms.

The subject of rights is beyond the scope of this book, except to encourage you to get a written agreement for all assignments, and don't be surprised if it feels like the magazine is asking for everything including rights to your first born child.

For example, a few years ago I wrote a Q & A type interview for a magazine who decided my questions weren't intrusive enough for their readers. Since I felt confident that the article was well written as it stood, I chose to not rewrite it, but to accept the kill fee and try to place it elsewhere, which I did. I received a verbal agreement from another magazine who was ready to pay me significantly more money than the first, with very little editing. I was thrilled ...

until I received the written contract confirming the sale.

The magazine was asking for every conceivable right, including some I had never even considered. I knew the article had the potential to be resold as a reprint in a number of different places so I wasn't too excited about signing the agreement. I called the editor, with whom I had a good rapport. The conversation went something like this:

"Hi Michael, this is Brad Swift. I'm calling about the contract I received from you today on the Lozoff interview, and I really have only one question: Do you ever get a writer to sign this thing?" I then chuckled a bit to take the edge off the question.

To my amazement, his reply was, "Well, we like to ask for everything, but if there's anything there that you don't feel is okay, feel free to mark through it."

That's what I did. By the time I sent the contract back, about half of it was crossed out, but they accepted it without a question. And yes, I did write for them again.

However, on other occasions I've tried to make much more subtle changes only to find that the magazine was completely inflexible. You never know until you ask.

Outlining and Questions

Once you've conferred with the editor and have received a written contract that everyone has signed, you're ready to get down to the joy of writing. Of course, all writers have their various approaches to the creative process, so I'll just talk about the one that works best for me.

I usually start with some form of an outline. Depending on my mood, I may start with a mind map type of outline, which is also known as clustering, or it may be a more standard outline of each section of the article as I see it.

My next step is to create a list of questions I need to answer that will form the content of the article. Since a lot of my articles have been either profiles, or other types of articles that involved interviewing people for most of the content, these questions form the basis for the interviews. Of course, I don't restrict myself to just these preliminary questions, but they do form the backbone of the interviews. Now, I'm ready for one of the most fun parts of the writing process – the interviews.

Setting Up and Conducting Interviews

The interviewing process is another area where new writers tend to have a lot of questions, so I'll see if I can't answer some of the most common ones here, starting with:

Do you get an okay from the subject first, or do you get an assignment first and then hope you can get the interview?

I've found it easiest to get the assignment first, which then makes it much easier to request and receive permission for the interview. Of course, this might be different if you're trying to interview Britney Spears or the Dali Lama, especially if the article you want to write is for your local hometown newspaper. But it's been my experience that people

90

want to be interviewed because they love to talk about themselves and their work or their area of expertise. In fact, if anything, I've found the bigger challenge is to keep the interview on track so that it doesn't get too involved or technical.

It also helps if you've done your homework before the interview. This may include researching the topic at your local library or through the Internet, and most certainly having a well prepared list of questions to work from. The last piece of the puzzle to bring to the interview is a genuine interest and curiosity about the subject. Once again, this is where writing about topics that you're passionate about helps a lot.

Other Kinds of Research

Interviews lend credibility to your article, but not all of your research will be done this way. Other sources may include material taken from research and/or trade journals, newspapers, books, and even the encyclopedia. A few words of caution: Information about almost anything is readily available on the Internet, but it's vital to make sure that your sources are reliable and accurate. Fact-checking is critical, and you should also include a list of your sources to the editor, because the magazine will probably want to do some of their own fact-checking. This isn't because they doubt your research, but the magazine needs to cover itself legally. This is again where talking to experts can be quite valuable, since they can often verify whether something you've come across from another source is true or not.

The First Draft

"When do you know that's it's time to start writing the article?" Believe it or not, that's a good and common question. I've found as I go through the research phase of the writing process, there comes a point where I start hearing myself say, "How am I going to get all this great material into this one article?" And that's a sure sign that I'm ready to write the rough draft. It doesn't necessarily mean I'm completely done with the research. I may find as I get into the draft that there are some holes in my research that need to be filled. That's fine. In most cases, I simply make a note of them and keep on writing, unless the hole is too big and the rest of the article hinges on filling it first.

There's an important distinction to make here that I've found can help many writers with the age old dilemma of 'writer's block.' And that's to remember that there's two parts to completing an article. There's the writing and then there's the editing or polishing. And the two mix about as well as oil and water. However, many writers insist on trying to make them mix, so they start their first sentence but even before they get to the end of it, their editor has turned itself on. "That's not the word you want. Why are you starting the article off like that? Are you sure that's the right punctuation. Is that really the way you spell "disassociation?" And on and on it goes, so that an hour later you're still on the first paragraph.

My approach that seems to work well is to place my outline next to my computer where I can see it, and my notes beside me to refer to, and to sit down and write the whole article as fast as I can while writing as well and as clearly as possible… without editing. I know that the first draft is far from being the final draft. It's likely I'll edit, polish, proof and re-edit it a number of times. I also know that I'm just part of a team producing this article, and that I'm first and foremost the writer, and that there's another person on the team who is first and foremost the editor, and that's why I'm called a writer and the other person is called an editor.

Keeping these two different roles in mind goes along way towards keeping me from taking the editing process personal. Of course, as with most things in life, there are exceptions and times when it's appeared to me that an editor has gone overboard with their job, and in those times I don't have a problem taking these matters up with the editor. The relationship between and writer and editor is similar in some ways to a marriage. In even the best of marriages there are times when the two people involved don't agree, and yet they are willing to work through those times because they know the overall relationship is worth it. The same is true with writers and editors. Don't be too quick to throw in the towel. Some of my best learning experiences, many of which I've shared in this book, have come from the disagreements I've had with editors.

Revisions

Whenever possible, I schedule my writing schedule on an assignment to allow a few days between the initial rough draft and the revision process. This is time to step away from the project so you can look at the draft with a fresh and hopefully more objective approach. It's also the time to do some follow up research to fill any of the holes that I came across during the rough draft stage.

It's at this stage that I take off my writer's hat and put on my editor's visor. I start by looking at the big picture. Is this the best lead I know with which to start the article? Is the outline of the article clear and does it flow well and in a logical sequence or could the paragraphs be rearranged in some way? Do I have the most pertinent and interesting material from my research in the article or did I drop out some of the meatier material? Is the ending really as strong as it could be?

From the bigger picture I begin to focus in on the finer details. One of the best ways I know to do this is to read the article out loud to myself. Many of the smaller errors, can be picked up easily this way. And, of course, I also utilize my word processor spell and grammar checker. Depending on the article and how I'm doing with my time frame I may go through this revision process two or three different times, with a day or two between each one.

Submission

"When do you know when the article is ready to be submitted?" Ahh, another great question. I know many writers, including myself, whose tendency towards perfectionism can result in a reluctance to submit the manuscript to the editor. Instead, they get caught in a revision vicious circle, until finally at the eleventh hour of the deadline, they

FedEx the package to their editor and then spend the next several nights tossing and turning about how they should have written the piece.

This is a sure sign that the writer has forgotten that he or she is part of a team, and that their primary role on the team is to come up with great ideas that they can write about, to write them, do their best to edit them, and to then turn them over to their editor to complete the process.

My general rule is to go through the revision and polishing process no more than three times. After that, it's time to put the article to rest and to turn it over to my partner, the editor, and to get on with my next assignment.

Call to Action Assignment

Take one of your best query ideas, and write a story as though you already had an assignment. While this is a fairly involved assignment, it will be well worth it. It will help build your confidence that you really can write a quality assignment, plus it's likely you'll also be able to find a home for it at some time in the future.

BONUS: Share your completed assignment with other writers and ask for the following feedback:

1. What works about this article?
2. What would you suggest changing that would make it stronger?
3. What magazine(s) do you feel would be interested in such an article?

Chapter 9
Counting the Cash

You've taken all the steps necessary to become a published and profitable writer – you've built your Taffy Machine, developed your Heart List, written dozens of queries, received some interesting assignments, and delivered quality articles to your assigning editors. Your byline now appears in your dream magazines. All of that means you're published, but what about the profitable part?

Let's talk a little bit about money issues.

Now that the article is written and submitted, when will I get paid?

The short answer to this question is, "it depends." One of the things it depends upon is whether the policy of the magazine is to pay on acceptance or on publication. Being paid on acceptance is preferred by most writers since it means you receive your check fairly soon after the article has been finished and approved by the editor. However, some publishers prefer waiting until after your article has appeared in their magazine, which may be months, years or even in a few cases, never.

Before you write the article, you should determine how and when the magazine pays. Ask your editor, and ask if you need to take any special steps to facilitate the payment process. Some magazines require that you submit an invoice with the article. If that's a requirement you fail to follow, you can slow the timing down by months.

If you haven't received a check within a reasonable amount of time after the due date, say 10 days or so, it's time to email or call your editor. Most editors aren't in control of the purse strings, but they can go to bat for you. Most magazines are careful to be sure their writers are paid on time, but just like everything in life, there are exceptions. If a magazine regularly delays your payments, you may want to examine whether or not you continue to write for them. Approach this as any other business would – if you don't make your car payments on time, the bank won't let you keep the car. If you don't pay your electric bill on time, the power company turns off your lights. If a magazine doesn't compensate you in a timely manner for the product you provide them, decide whether or not it's worth it to your business to continue to writing for them.

What is writing on spec and why should I avoid it?
Spec stand for 'speculation' and writing an article on spec means you agree to write the article hoping and praying that when it's done and if the editor likes it, and if they have room for it in their magazine, and if the moon is full, then they might decide to pay you for it. In my opinion, offering to write on spec or accepting such a request tags you as a rank amateur, and should be done ... well, never.

"But what if I am a rank amateur?" I hear you ask. Well, the first person you need to convince that this really isn't true is yourself, and one of the ways to do this is to act like a professional writer, and professional writers don't write on spec.

The only exceptions would be in the realm of personal essays or fiction, which are only accepted after they're written. There are also some small niche magazines that only accept articles on spec, but that have such impressive reputations that writing for them is a feather in your cap. But those are few and far between.

What are the different ways of being paid?

The most common ways of being paid are:

- per word,
- per page,
- per column inch, or
- flat fee

Many magazines will list their payment scale in their writers guidelines as paying a certain amount per word, typically anywhere between five cents and a dollar per word or more. However, don't get caught up in the game of counting every word. When the contract arrives, it will usually state a specific amount they're paying that is calculated on the pay/word count. For example, a magazine might say, "We pay $1 per word" in their guidelines and when you receive the contact it might say, "Payment will be $800 for a 800 word article." Most magazines don't expect you to send in the article with exactly 800 words but you should work to have it as close to that as possible.

While being paid per page isn't as common, some magazines do use this approach. Of course, it makes sense to know what size page they're talking about and how many words their pages average. In this way, you can convert this payment approach to a good estimate for what it would be on pay per word scale.

Newspapers usually base their pay rates on the column inch. By determining the average number of words per column inch you can convert to a pay per word scale and compare apples to apples.

A flat rate scale is fairly common, especially for short pieces and articles for departmental areas of the magazine that have a standard word count.

The last point I'd like to make is to not just look at the payment method and rate, but also look at the amount of time you'll need to devote to writing the article. Some articles require a lot more research, or the editors are more demanding and therefore you can end up spending more time in rewrites. This can result in what may appear as a very good pay per word scale being not nearly as good a payment per hour scale, which is really what you as a professional writer should keep in mind. After all, there are only so many hours in a day to write, so you want to leverage this time as much as possible.

For example, I have a publication that I've enjoyed writing for more than ten years, even though they pay a flat rate of $300 per article. Here's why I enjoy writing for them:

- The articles are easy to query, and most often the ideas come from the work I do as a coach.
- The articles themselves require little, if any research, since most of the content comes from my own business experience and expertise. I

can complete most of them in less than 2 hours, counting polishing and submitting.

- The editors are great to work with and after they edit my pieces they always read much better.
- The articles also serve as excellent marketing for one of my coaching niches, so I'm getting paid for my marketing efforts.
- Last but not least, I can often recycle the articles for my own electronic newsletter and from time to time resell them to other business magazines.

So while the pay scale based on the word count or the flat rate would suggest this is a low paying market, when I take everything into consideration, for me this is a great market.

If I'm just getting started should I consider writing for free?
This question isn't an easy one to answer. It really does depend on the writer and the situation. While I strongly recommend to not write on spec, there are a few forms of writing for no pay that can be used to move you forward in your writing career, or that can inspire you to continue writing until the checks begin to flow in. Some of these include writing your own electronic newsletters, which is a form of marketing; writing for publications and organizations that you believe in and that are aligned with your values, which would be considered a charitable donation; and exchanging your writing

talents for other services which you can use, which is bartering.

Even though I've made thousands of dollars from my writing through the years, in 1997 I started writing for free by publishing my own electronic newsletter, or ezine, entitled Purposeful Pondering Ezine. If you'd like to subscribe you can go to: www.lifeonpurpose.com.

Purposeful Pondering Ezine has become not only a great way for me to express myself and my life purpose, but has also become a foundational piece of Life On Purpose Institute's cybercommunity. And the truth is that it's not really writing for free. From the ezine, I receive a steady stream of new coaching clients and participants for the Life On Purpose programs. It's just that I don't get paid by the publication for each article I write.

You may also find it beneficial to write for other publications and organizations that you believe in, either for the pure pleasure of making a contribution with your words, or to help promote yourself as a writer or some other kind of expert. Article writing has many benefits beyond just receiving a check in the mail. The main point is to be clear that you are maintaining a certain energetic balance, that there's a steady exchange of value in both directions.

This is also true for bartering your writing talents. Be sure that the product or service you receive in return is something that you value and that you can use. Bartering arrangements where both parties feel justly compensated are the ones that work. All too often, in a desire to get something for our efforts, we can sell ourselves short. Don't do it. Writing is an art form that has immense value. Enjoy and benefit from your gift.

What are some simple strategies for financial record keeping?

The number one strategy is to be sure that you have some simple and effective system for keeping track of your income and expenses. If you view your writing as a business and not as a hobby, you'll be well on your way to being truly profitable. Invest in a simple accounting program like Quicken and use it.

An important part of running a business is to set aside time to "work on the business" as well as "work in the business." Working on the business includes setting up and maintaining systems that help you become more effective and efficient. That's what the Writers Taffy Machine is. It's a marketing system. You need the same type of system to manage your finances.

I also encourage you to set a goal to hire a bookkeeper within the first year of your writing business. Sure, you can keep track of your financial books by yourself but is that really how your want to invest your time? Why not pay someone $15 to $30 an hour so you can use that time doing what you really love doing – writing? You can make far more than $30 an hour if you devote that time to marketing and writing.

Call to Action Assignment

Spend an hour this week learning about financial record keeping systems, then set a goal to create your own within the next two weeks.

BONUS: Set a goal to hire a part time bookkeeper within the first year of your business.

Chapter 10 -- The Power of Words to Create a Life On Purpose

"Words do not label things already there. Words are like the knife of the carver: They free the idea, the thing, from the general formlessness of the outside. As a man speaks, not only is his language in a state of birth, but also the very thing about which he is talking." From an Old Eskimo saying

While we may often think that our words only have the power to describe something that is already real, I believe they have the power to literally create our world, to "free the idea, the thing, from the general formlessness of the outside." I believe that's what was meant by the famous saying, "the pen is mightier than the sword." As writers, we have the power to help create our world. This book is one of the ways that I have chosen to use this power, not only to create a world on purpose through my own words but to encourage you, the reader, to do the same in your own unique and authentic way.

Remember, while this book as been about helping you to fan your passion filled ideas into moneymaking magazine articles, making money has not been the only focus, nor really the primary one. Make a difference with your writing. Stretch yourself and stretch your readers with new ideas. Help to carve out our world. Make your time sitting at your keyboard count. If you do, you'll find that in the process you've been creating a life for yourself that matters -- a life on purpose.

Appendix A
Sample Query Letters

W. BRADFORD SWIFT DVM •

Omni Magazine
Ms.Erin Murphy

Dear Erin,

TOBACCO: WONDER PLANT OF THE NINETIES?

"It's not science fiction," says Raymond Long, professor of crop science at N. C. State University in Raleigh. "The potential is now there to grow an acre of tobacco and extract material for uses in food, drink, pharmaceuticals and other products."

It may be the ultimate story of turning lemons into lemonade. Tobacco, maligned for years for its cancer-causing properties, may one day soon be used as an economical source of high quality protein for food. Through biogenetic engineering, companies such as Biosource Genetics are turning tobacco plants into living factories for the cheap, mass production of such important compounds as anti-virus proteins and human blood proteins.

"The major one we got the plants to create was the anti-AIDS Compound Q," said Larry Grill, vice president of research for Biosource.

This could be the lead for my article on the breakthrough research being conducted to transform tobacco from mass murderer to savior.

Some of the key points that will be addressed in the article are:

• Tobacco: a source of high quality nutrition. Tobacco is capable of producing more protein biomass than any green plant including alfalfa. One of tobacco's proteins called Fraction-1 has higher nutritional value than the milk protein, casein, which is the standard by which other proteins' nutritional value is measured.
• Tobacco plants: living factories. Combining the unrivaled yields of tobacco with biogenetic engineering could turn tobacco plants into living factories capable of turning out cheap, mass produced industrial chemicals, medicines, and cosmetics.
• Economics is the key. According to experts such as Raymond Long, the technology is available to move the alternate uses of tobacco from the laboratory to the consumer. The question lies in the dollars and cents of it.

I'll use as resources for this article such experts as:

• Raymond Long, professor of crop science at N. C. State University. Long has conducted much of the research on finding alternate uses for tobacco.
• Biosource Genetics Corporation, a biotechnology firm in Vacaville, California. Biosource has patented a genetically altered virus that prompts tobacco leaves to make proteins on request including anti-AIDS Compound Q.

As a freelance writer with a strong science and medical background (see enclosed bio), I'll successfully translate the technical jargon of the research into the language of the

b

layman. This ability to take highly technical material and transform it into interesting and informative reading while capturing the human element of the story is what the editors of USAIR Magazine, Entrepreneur, Dog Fancy, Cat Fancy, and many others have come to expect from me.

Through the years, I've learned to only write on subjects about which I am passionate. The breakthrough research of Raymond Long and Biosource is very important to the economics of my home state of North Carolina-- their results will reach much further. I promise to deliver an article which your readers will not be able to put down.

Since this would be the first time I've had the pleasure to write for *Omni* , I would be happy to write this article on speculation. Would you agree your readers would enjoy learning about this botanical equivalent of Dr. Jekyll and Mr. Hyde? I look forward to your comments.

Sincerely,

Joe Editor
Very Large Magazine

Dear Joe,

On the trail, he was the leader of a partnership affectionately
known as the Orient Express. Together, he and his companion
Bill Irwin trekked the 2,168 miles of the Appalachian trail, a
journey which began in Springer Mountain, Georgia on March 8,
1990 and wouldn't end until Nov. 21 at Abol Bridge, Maine,
eight and a half months later.
During the year, 1450 other hikers would begin the journey.
Only 120 would finish. Of those, the Orient Express was a
unique team -- Bill, the first and only blind man to walk the
entire trial and Orient, his guide dog. This is Orient's story.

This could be my lead for one of the most miraculous and
moving stories of the 90's. At the time, it made national
headlines. Now, two years later, what impact has this
incredible journey had on Bill's and Orient's lives?

I had the opportunity to find out when I spent the day
with the two wanderers just two days before their second
anniversary commemorating the end of their historic trip.
I'd like to share their experience with your readers with
my article, "The Orient Express."

The article will focus on Orient, a gorgeous five-year old
German Shepherd Seeing Eye dog who recently won the "
1992 Hero Dog Award" from the German Shepherd Dog
Club of America.

Some of the main points that will be covered in the article
are:

d

- What were the special challenges that faced Orient during the eight and a half month journey?
- How did Bill manage the care and feeding of Orient during a trip where hypothermia as well as heat stroke and dehydration were just a few of the problems?
- How did Bill and Orient, both "city slickers" at heart, learn to cope with the wilderness of the Appalachian Trail?
- What has life "after the Trail" been like for Orient and what has opened up for the two adventurers?

My sources for the article will be from Bill Irwin and Orient who live close by in Burlington N. C. I'll also refer to their newsletter, "The Orient Express", which was started while they were on the trail with 70 subscribers and has now grown to over 3000 readers. I may also take a few quotes from Bill's recent book, Blind Courage, which was released late this summer.

I believe you're familiar with my writing background, having published several of my articles in the past. I feel I am in a unique position to write this article, being able to listen to Bill's account with a veterinarian's prospective. At the same time as a writer of fiction and non-fiction, I'll capture the special warmth and compassion of this incredible story.

Wouldn't you like to introduce your readers to this special dog and his owner? I'd enjoy the opportunity to make the introductions. I look forward to hearing your comments.

Sincerely,

• W. BRADFORD SWIFT DVM •

Susan Nice Person
Interesting Magazine Group
789 Reader's Row
Boston, Ma 12345

Dear Susan,

Bo Lozoff speaks in a soft voice but his message carries
loud and clear through out the packed auditorium at the
"Breaking Free" retreat in Black Mountain, North Carolina.
His message, "A Safer, Kinder Society" has an unexpected
edge to it.
As he sits crossed-legged on a table so to be clearly seen by
everyone, his words bite through the crisp mountain air,
"If 'faggot, nigger, dike' hurts you, then scum-sucking,
sleeze-bag, criminal hurts me because I've never met one
and I've been in hundreds and hundreds of prisons, and
right now the manager of our 'Kindness House' is
someone who served ten years in prison for murder. . . "

This might be the lead paragraph for a profile on Bo
Lozoff, the founder of The Human Kindness Foundation in
Durham, North Carolina, who with his wife, Sita, have
devoted more than twenty years of their lives to create a
safer kinder society through their tireless efforts.

The article will highlight the four primary projects which
are at the heart of The Human Kindness Foundation. They
are:

• The Prison-Ashram Project which was started with the
help of Ram Daas 22 years ago in which prison time is

f

transformed from a time of punishment into an opportunity for spiritual searching and growth.

• Bo's lecture series, which focuses on two main topics: service as a lifestyle and the urgent need to create a safer kinder society by reforming the prison system from a punitive system to a reparative system.

• Books and tapes, most of which were written by Bo and published by The Human Kindness Foundation. Hundreds of these books and tapes are mailed out free of charge each month to prisoners participating in the Prison-Ashram Project.

• Kindness House, the newest project, was opened this past May when the one of the Foundation's supporter donated over $120,000 for its purchase. Prisoners who have found value from the other projects can come to Kindness House upon their release for up to a year. The time qualifies as a legitimate parole plan and gives the ex-prisoners an opportunity to give back to other prisoners by assisting with the daily maintenance of the Prison-Ashram Project.

One of Bo's main points in his lectures on prison reform is that our present system of punishing law-breakers which we've put in place to reduce crime may actually be creating more criminals since currently two-thirds of the prison population is composed of offenders of non- violent crimes but who are mixed indiscriminately with the other one-third who are dangerous, violent people. As Bo points out, "When you place 66 non-violent people with 34 violent people for five or ten years, what you end up with are 100 violent people who are likely to break the law again and again."

His plea for a reparative system of prison reform is gathering support. Bo cites such notables as Larry Mechum, Commissioner of Corrections for Connecticut and Janet Reno, current Attorney General and a member of "Campaign for an Effective Crime Policy, who agree that such a transformation is desperately needed.

Besides further interviews with Bo and Seta for this article, I'll also stay at Kindness House and participate as a volunteer to gather a true sense of the efforts of The Human Kindness Foundation.

Over the past 13 years as a freelance writer, profiles such as the one I'm recommending on Bo have become one of my favorite types of articles. I'm currently working on Project Purpose, to write 100 profiles about people who lives are directed by their purpose or vision. You can count on me to capture more than just the facts, but also the many facets of a man who has given himself over to a life of service. My articles have appeared in a diverse collection of magazines including <u>Entrepreneur, Omni,</u> <u>Better Homes and Garden</u> and <u>Family Fun,</u> to name a few.

I can have a finished 1500 - 2000 word article on your desk within 45 days of being given the assignment. Interested? I'll follow up within the next ten days to answer any questions you may have and if your like, create a top-notch article with you.

Sincerely,

h

Jim Editor
National Pet Magazine
1234 Purina St.
Big City, NY 12598

Dear Jim:

A ONE WOMAN CANINE CRUSADE"

She stands just 4' 11" and weighs in at less than a hundred
and ten pounds, but if you're an owner of a junkyard in
Harlem and you're abusing your dog, you'd rather deal
with Charles Bronson then Chitra Besbroda.

While most people think of junkyard dogs as filthy,
snarling beasts to be avoided at all cost, Chitra knows from
20 years of experience that they are helpless, abused
animals in desperate need of food, water and love.

I'm proposing an article entitled, A ONE WOMAN
CANINE CRUSADE, a heart wrenching and yet also a
heart-warming story of one woman's stand to make a
difference under some of the most difficult conditions
imaginable.

Chitra Besbroda is the creator of "Sentient Creatures," a
non-profit organization dedicated to the rescue,
rehabilitation and placement of junkyard dogs and public
education about pets' rights. Wading through rusted car
parts, broken glass and other filth which makes up the
dog's normal environment, Chitra has rescued over 1600
dogs from the junkyards of Harlem in the twenty years
she's been waging her campaign.

i

Although the plight of these animals will tear at the heart strings of the most cynical person, Chitra's story is ultimately one of inspiration and courage; a demonstration of the difference one person can make when they are committed to something larger than themselves.

If you're looking for a non-partial report on this story, I'm not the writer to cover it. As a veterinarian for 15 years prior to becoming a full time writer, my heart ached during the initial phone conversation with Chitra, as she shared the inhumane treatment these pets suffer at the hands of their owners. At the same time, 1600+ dogs now have wonderful homes with plenty to eat, warm places to sleep and families that love them. It's this sharp contrast which makes this such a strong story... Interested?

Sincerely,

W. Bradford Swift, DVM

Life On Purpose Institute
A LIFE ON PURPOSE IS A LIFE OF SERVICE, SIMPLICITY AND
SERENITY

Sally Editor
Inspirational Stories Magazine
8910 Feel Good Drive
Happy City, MD 78234

Dear Sally:

Untroubled Youth

I received a special package in the mail a few weeks ago
from someone I've only had the pleasure of meeting by
phone. In the package was a book written by this young
man, plus a brochure of the nonprofit organization he co-
founded in 1990 and a short yet powerful bio with the
following credentials:

• Organized first peace march at age 7.
• Ran first marathon at 10.
• Opened his first business, "Oceans Natural Bakery," at
about the same time, selling his goodies door-to-door to
hundreds of his neighbors.
• Facilitated two international youth summits in Moscow
and in Washington D. C. at age 14 and 15.

"My God, his dad must be proud of him," was my first
thought. Then, the next night while watching the 48-Hours
Special on the Class of the Year 2000, I was struck once

k

more how unlike the typical teenager Ocean Robbins has been. It's not surprising that with a name like "Ocean" and a father like activist and author, John Robbins, this young man would have a keen interest in the environment. Unlike many of his peers who have become resigned that they can't make a difference, Robbins decided he could and would.

At 15, he formed the Creating Our Future environmental speaking tour, during which he and three other participants spoke to over 30,000 students. He then co-founded Youth for Environmental Sanity (YES!), which he directed for five years. So far, YES! has reached over a half-million students in over 1200 schools in 38 states, as well as organizing 20 summer camps in 6 countries, and has grown to a viable non-profit organization with an annual budget over $250,000.

The book Robbins sent me, *Choices For Our Future: A Generation Rising for Life on Earth*, has sold over 15,000 copies since being published in 1994. Robbins is now 23 years old, and already he has made a profound difference with a segment of our culture known for their cynicism and despair — the youth of America. His life is in sharp contrast with the lives of his peers depicted in the 48-Hours show, where drugs and an indifferent attitude are par for the course.

This contrast might be the focus of the profile article I'm proposing. Some of the main points that will be covered are:

• What kind of background and child rearing led to young Robbins' positive attitude and actions? His dad, John Robbins, is a noted author and activist I've interviewed before and will interview again for this piece, along with Ocean's mother, Deo Robbins.

• What was his inspiration and motivation behind starting YES! and what are its central goals?

• What has been the reception Robbins has received from his peers as he and his partners have gone into the schools to speak on environmental issues? How does he motivate young people? Obviously, something has been working. His work has inspired over 110 new Environmental Clubs to be started and his organization has received more than 8,000 letters from students requesting additional support.

• What is Robbins' outlook on the future given the current environmental and political trends?

I'm currently working on my pet writing project, PROJECT PURPOSE: To write 100+ articles about people and institutions whose lives are dedicated to a bold and inspired purpose or vision. Out of this project has grown The Life On Purpose Foundation, a nonprofit organization whose purpose is to acknowledge and promote such people as Ocean Robbins. I'm including a couple clips from Project Purpose.

If you agree a profile on Ocean and YES! would be of interest and inspiration to *ICON* readers, perhaps in your "A Glance" section, say YES! and I can have a completed article on your desk within 45-days.

Sincerely,

m

www.ingramcontent.com/pod-product-compliance
Lightning Source LLC
Chambersburg PA
CBHW031211270326
41931CB00006B/518